GRACIOUS
IMPERATIVES

GRACIOUS IMPERATIVES

Discipleship Toward the 21st Century

BRIAN KELLEY BAUKNIGHT

ABINGDON PRESS
Nashville

GRACIOUS IMPERATIVES

Copyright © 1992 by Abingdon Press

This book is printed on recycled, acid-free paper.

Library of Congress Cataloging-in-Publication Data

BAUKNIGHT, BRIAN KELLEY, 1939-
  Gracious imperatives : discipleship toward the 21st century / Brian Kelley Bauknight.
    p.   cm.
  Includes bibliographical references.
  ISBN 0-687-15677-7 (alk. paper)
    1. Christian life—1960 - 2. Bauknight, Brian Kelley, 1939-
  I. Title
  BV4501.2.B3845156   1992
  248.4—dc20   91-21859
                                                            CIP

Scripture quotations, unless otherwise indicated, are from the New Revised Standard Version Bible, copyright © 1989, by the Division of Christian Education of the National Council of the Churches of Christ in the United States of America.

Scripture quotations noted GNB are from the *Good News Bible*—Old Testament: Copyright © American Bible Society 1976; New Testament: Copyright © American Bible Society 1966, 1971, 1976. Used by permission.

MANUFACTURED IN THE UNITED STATES OF AMERICA

In memory of my father

Wilfred Bauknight

*whose vision of the church nurtured my vision,
and whose love of good preaching
prods me on toward the best utilization
of the gifts God gives*

CONTENTS

Introduction... 9

For Thanksgiving:
   1. Give Thanks!..13

For Advent:
   2. Stay Awake!...19
   3. Journey Gently!..................................... 27
   4. Bring Light!...35
   5. Grasp Hope!... 41

For Christmas Eve:
   6. Would You Like to Hold the Baby?.............47

For the New Year and Beyond:
   7. Maintain Vision!.................................... 53
   8. Cultivate Compassion!..............................61
   9. Focus Inward!...................................... 69
   10. Worship Faithfully!................................ 77
   11. Pursue Perfection!................................. 85
   12. Spread Encouragement!..............................93
   13. Sustain Spirituality!..............................101

Notes.. 109

INTRODUCTION

The Christian community is in desperate need of some definitive ingredients for discipleship as we head toward the twenty-first century. We flounder and grope for a clearer vision of what it means to be both a vital, living church and faithful disciples of Jesus Christ. No emerging vision can any longer be stated in absolute terms. Nor can it be formulated in a negative framework, such as that of the Ten Commandments. The call toward discipleship must find new words, new expression, and be overflowing with grace. Additionally, that call must connect meaningfully with the real lives of real persons. And it must always recognize that each pilgrim will be at a slightly different stage on the journey.

During a recent personal retreat period, I began to recognize—essentially for the first time—how much wise counsel in the letters to the early churches began with a gracious invitation, "Let us. . . . " As I began to search, I found more than a dozen such clear and helpful pieces. I also found some powerful verses that, while not specifically beginning with these two words, had the same gracious invitation clearly implied. Each one seemed to be integral to the formative life of the early church. When collected and examined prayerfully, these verses became an expression of discipleship that captured my attention and my heart.

The title of this book is indicative of my own theological stance. The imperatives are "gracious" because of God's divinely originated care for us and for our lives. Prevenient grace is a pillar of my understanding of the nature of God. The words are "imperative" because of their urgency and their clear relationship to who we are and what God asks of us in response to abounding grace.

There are clearly more "gracious imperatives" than are contained in this one small volume. Consider a few other textual gems:

Let us run with perseverance the race that is set before us. (Heb. 12:1) [*run steadily!*]

[Let us] give . . . not reluctantly or under compulsion, for God loves a cheerful giver. (II Cor. 9:7) [*give cheerfully!*]

Beloved, let us love one another. (I John 4:7) [*love actively!*]

So let us not grow weary in doing what is right. (Gal. 6:9) [*maintain righteousness!*]

I even considered one thoughtful imperative in the beautiful Christmas Eve text: "Let us go now to Bethlehem and see this thing that has taken place" (Luke 2:15). Others are waiting to be unearthed. The list might prove virtually inexhaustible. Gracious imperatives all!

I am deeply grateful to the selection committee of the United Methodist segment of the Protestant Hour for their confidence in choosing me to deliver these words over the radio. I am awed to stand in the long line of those who have made an enormous contribution to the work of the gospel through this channel for nearly fifty years.

I celebrate the members and friends of Christ Church who have encouraged and challenged me in the long hours of preparation, refinement, and reflection. I rejoice in a staff of lay and clergy colleagues who love me and who believe that this process will strengthen my ministry and the local church to which I am appointed. I am especially thankful to David Caldwell and Judy Steeb from that staff, who carefully proofread the written text and made suggestions. I express deep gratitude to my wife, Elaine, who celebrated this opportunity with me and who—during the many hours of writing and rewriting—gave me space, encouragement, and support.

These messages are extended to you out of a lifelong love for the local church. The book is dedicated to the memory of my father, who—without either of us knowing the outcome at the time—gave me absolute, unwavering confidence that the church is God's best hope for a sane and stable world.

The good news of the gospel is the best news there is. The Christian journey is an amazing adventure under abounding grace. May spiritual blessings and peace in abundance rest upon each reader of this little volume.

Brian Kelley Bauknight
Christ United Methodist Church
Bethel Park, Pennsylvania
February 1991

GIVE THANKS!

Let us give thanks. . . .   (HEB. 12:28)

Someone has said that God has two dwelling places. One is in heaven, and the other is in a thankful heart. This is the season to remember that legacy of wisdom.

In the earliest memories of my childhood, I find constant reminders to give thanks. "Thank you" for a special treat. "Thank you" for Christmas and birthday gifts. "Thank you for letting me play at your house." "Thank you" at brief mealtime prayers. The imperative gradually extended everywhere. A first order of life, of friendship, of etiquette, and of prayer was "thank you!" The memory of such instruction still permeates my life.

To give thanks was a distinct responsibility in my home. Yet, it was always enjoined in the spirit of grace. Never a law, it was always opportunity.

This chapter and the ones that follow will focus on a number of similar imperatives for the Christian journey. We shall discover instructions that come out of the New Testament letters from Paul and others. They guided the life of the early church, and they clearly extend into our lives in this last decade of the twentieth century.

God's gracious imperatives begin with gratitude, which is at the heart of the life of the disciple. "Let us be grateful," writes the author of Hebrews. "Let us give thanks, by which we offer to God an acceptable worship with reverence and awe" (Heb. 12:28).

Thanks may be the most valuable word in any language. It is said that when Mark Twain was at the peak of his career, his writing was valued at five dollars per word. Some college prankster wrote Twain a letter, saying, "Dear Mr. Twain: enclosed is $5. Please send me your best word." Shortly, a reply came. It simply said, "Thanks!"

Thanks is a word that rises to the surface in our lives these days. It is a word that has several levels—all of which are important to us.

Thankfulness Toward One Another

At one level, *thanks* is a word we need to speak to one another. It is an important word of affirmation and appreciation. Sometimes, it may be a simple word to a bank teller, a grocery bagger, a waitress, or an oil change mechanic. *Thank you* are healing words, kind words.

Most of us know how good it feels to receive gratitude. Such affirmation is important to our completeness, our health and wholeness as human beings. It is equally crucial—a gracious imperative of Christian living—that we send our word of thanks into our world. "Thanks" must be frequently spoken and heard. To live thankfully toward one another is healthy—mentally, emotionally, and spiritually.

Not long ago, I heard a wonderful story about a group of people who were gathered for a reunion during the Thanksgiving season. They were mid-life adults remembering persons in their personal histories. One member of the group said, "Well, I for one am grateful for Mrs. Simpson, a school teacher I had in a little West Virginia town thirty years ago. She went out of her way to introduce me to Tennyson."

He then launched into a colorful description of this woman who had made an obvious impression on his life. She had carefully and creatively awakened his literary interest and developed his gifts for expression.

"And does Mrs. Simpson know that she made such a contribution to your life?" another asked.

"I'm afraid she doesn't," he replied. "I never told her."

"Why don't you write her?" came the response.

The challenge was accepted, even though he had no assurance his former teacher was still alive. That night, this man—now balding and in his early forties—sat down and wrote his teacher of many years ago a Thanksgiving letter.

It took about a week for the post office to search out Mrs. Simpson. The letter was forwarded from town to town. Finally, it reached her, and the following handwritten note came by return mail.

My dear Willie:

I remember well your enthusiasm for Tennyson and the *Idylls of the King* when I read them to you, for you were so beautifully responsive. My reward for telling you about Tennyson did not have to wait until your belated note of thanks came to me in my old age. I received my best reward in your eager response to the lyrical beauty and the idealism of Tennyson.

You will be interested to know that I taught school for fifty years and, in all that time, yours is the first note of appreciation I ever received. It came on a blue, cold morning, and it cheered my lonely old heart as nothing has cheered me in many years.

Here was the power of a "thank you" for both the giver and the receiver. It lifted both lives to a new level of wholeness—the wholeness that is exactly the goal God has in mind for our lives. It would mean a great deal if each of us would write two or three short notes of gratitude to a few unthanked contributors to our own pilgrimage during the coming Thanksgiving season.

Thankfulness Toward Life

At a second level, *thanks* is a word we need to speak to life itself. We need a greater attitude of gratitude toward the very matter of being alive.

Two films of recent years come to mind. The first is *The Milagro Beanfield War*—a story that opens with the awakening of a very old man at the dawn of a new day. He crawls out of bed, stiffly and in some pain, totters over to a mirror in his small cottage, looks at his reflection, and then says, "Thank you, God, for another day of life."

An even more powerful example comes in the 1986 film, *The Trip to Bountiful,* for which Geraldine Page won an Academy Award. Miss Page plays the part of an aging mother living with her son and daughter-in-law in a tiny, cramped house in Houston in the late 1940s. Her chief goal in her old age is to return once more to Bountiful, Texas, to the little town and land and house of her childhood.

As the story unfolds, she makes her way back to this town by grace, grit, and sheer determination. But Bountiful has died. The little store is closed, the land is no longer producing, and her childhood home is vacant and falling into ruin. A bit saddened, but undeterred, she celebrates the fact that she has come home—for an hour.

Quickly, the viewers of the film realize that the true "bountiful" is the "bountiful" of the heart. The woman's face and heart are replete with gratitude. Quietly, she scoops up a handful of soil and lets it fall again. As she leaves, she says, "I am so happy, so content." A psalm of thanksgiving to life and for life is forever etched upon her heart.

When I was a child, my sisters, my mother and I made an annual pilgrimage every summer to a little town in Tennessee that was the home of my maternal grandparents. Each summer was a great adventure: aunts and uncles, distant cousins, grandparents, and relatives whose connection to the family I never did learn. There was an old barn sitting on a few acres of ground with some chickens, a couple of pigs, a cow, and an old mule. There was always a large garden and a well for fresh water. An outhouse completed the landscape of this memory.

How I loved those two weeks on that Tennessee hill. I could sit on the porch with my grandfather in silence for hours; or I could help my grandmother churn butter. I felt rich and full and blessed. And I was.

It was only after I became an adult that I realized how poor my grandparents really were, for they were sharecroppers. They had no social security, no income, only the house and the land. It was sheer simplicity of life, but it seemed bountiful and beautiful to me—and it was!

When we can say "thank you" for life, we are healthier, happier, and more whole. Yet, do we not have a strange twisting of our values today? Instead of gratitude, we insist on entitlement. I am entitled to a good wage, to two weeks vacation, to a company car. I am entitled to upward mobility, to a higher standard of living, to my parents' inheritance. I am entitled to a college education, and to a down payment for my first house. I am entitled to the bedroom furniture from my room in the home where I grew up.

It is not so much that we might not be given some of these things anyway by those who love us. Frequently that does happen. The issue, however, is the mood of entitlement. And thanks is scarce.

A corporate executive said to me recently, "We must prepare ourselves and our children to live a less affluent life-style *and still be grateful!*" His words are prophetic for the twenty-first century.

Thanksgiving to life and for life is losing ground. To recover it is to recover something uniquely valuable for authentic living.

Thankfulness Toward God

The deepest level of thankfulness is thanksgiving rendered directly to God. This is the thanksgiving that draws all of life together. It is not enough to be generically thankful to life. Life finds its fullness only when we say, "Thanks be to God!" Such thanksgiving is beyond politeness, beyond protocol, and beyond personal gratitude to one another. Its focus is God.

Yet, again, we are in some trouble. In our societal drift toward secularization and self-interest, we are losing our capacity to give thanks to God. We are so preoccupied with outside stimuli, so busy with daily living, so cluttered with schedules, that we can no longer remember to be grateful to God for all that is. The Deuteronomic warning in the Old Testament is very contemporary: "Take care that you do not forget!" (Deut. 6:12).

"Thank you, God" is a prayer we need to relearn. Consider this for a moment: Who will say the thanksgiving prayer at your household table on Thanksgiving Day? Where is the individual or family member or extended family member who knows how to express thanks to God for thirty seconds or so?

A theologian once said, "Thanksgiving is consecration; it transforms something secular into the sphere of the holy." The secular crowds us. It confuses us, controls the larger part of us, and eventually edges God out.

One of the great hymns of this season was written by Martin Rinkart in the early seventeenth century during the Thirty Years' War. Rinkart pastored a city of refuge during the war. There was terrible pestilence and famine. He buried over four thousand persons in one year, including several members of his own family. Yet, in the midst of such tragedy and pain, he wrote:

> Now thank we all our God, with heart and hands and voices,
> Who wondrous things has done, in whom this world rejoices;
> Who from our mothers' arms has blessed us on our way
> With countless gifts of love, and still is ours today.

God's urgent and gracious imperative is for a life centered in thanksgiving. We remember the awesome power of thanksgiving. We remember the grace of a thankful heart.

To say "thank you" at each deepening level of life is to draw us closer to the One who is the Source and Sustainer of life. One good word will do it. "Thanks!" But with a clear and certain focus: "Thanks be to God!" Today and always.

C H A P T E R 2

Stay Awake!

So then let us not fall asleep as others do, but let us keep awake and be sober.   (I THESS. 5:6)

This verse is an auspicious beginning for reflection. Paul writes, "So then let us not fall asleep." What a marvelous challenge with which to begin a message!

In one congregation, a man was notorious for sleeping through the sermon every week. Finally, the preacher decided to find a remedy. As he drew his sermon to a close one Sunday, he issued a loud and directed call to the congregation: "Everybody who wants to go to heaven, stand up!"

Naturally, everyone stood—that is, everyone except the man who was sawing logs in the corner. Whereupon the preacher called, "Harry, are you asleep?"

"No, Preacher, I'm not sleeping," came the muffled reply.

"Well, Harry, didn't you hear what I just said to the people?"

"Yes, Preacher, I heard."

"Well? Don't you want to go to heaven?"

"Oh, yes sir, Preacher, I want to go to heaven."

"Well, then, why didn't you stand?"

"Oh well, Preacher, I guess I thought you were getting up a load to go now!"

So, then, let us not fall asleep!

These words are also a great text for the beginning of the Advent season: "Let us not fall asleep as others do, but let us keep awake and be sober." The function of Advent is much like Lent. It is a time for reflection, for focusing, and, possibly, for the discipline of fasting. It is one of two times during the Christian year when we are called to some critical fine-tuning of our spiritual selves. During Advent, we have four weeks of keen preparation for receiving the great good news one more time.

Finally, this text is also good for guiding general discipleship. In this chapter, we will look at the two strongly positive imperatives in this text: "keep awake" and "be sober."

Be Sober!

First, let us look at the matter of sobriety. This issue is larger than alcohol or even drugs—although it certainly encompasses both. The Apostle means here that we are to be fully functional, as God gives us capacity. He is saying, "Be at your maximum, in accordance with all that God has given you."

The dictionary defines *sober* as being "temperate," and *temperate* is defined as "moderation as to the indulgence of appetites." Such moderation in our indulgence is very important during the Advent season.

What a contradiction we truly are as human beings, and even as Christians. We frequently observe Advent in exactly the opposite fashion. Food and alcohol are consumed in greater quantities during Advent than at any other time of the year. The lines at the liquor stores are longer. The traffic jams at supermarkets are massive. We buy regular foods and specialty foods and ingredients for baking in abundance. Even if we have a fairly modest social calendar during the other months of the year, we have a busy calendar during December—and most of those events are filled with excesses of food and drink.

At the very time when the cycle of the Christian year calls us to be at our best—to be lean and keen—we eat and drink to excess. We get physically, mentally, and spiritually flabby. It is almost as though we have some obligation to lose control.

Part of the tragedy in all of this is that such over-indulgence is not easily reversed. Anyone who has tried to shed the few extra pounds of weight put on during the holidays knows the truth of this statement!

I am told that a recovering alcoholic or drug addict must allow at least twelve months for his or her system to cleanse itself of the chemical dependency. The substances and their effects remain in our bodies, after total cessation of use, for up to twelve months or more.

Perhaps this is why there is such an urgency in Paul's tone here. We must begin early and quickly. Jesus speaks with similar urgency: "Be on guard so that your hearts are not weighed down with dissipation and drunkenness" (Luke 21:34).

Consider the words around the anticipation of the birth of John the Baptist. The messenger says to John's father, "He [John] must never drink wine or strong drink" (Luke 1:15). More than a commitment to total abstinence, this is a symbol of the need for the fullest kind of sobriety in relation to the preparation for the coming of Christ. This is careful and deliberate preaching by Luke as he tells us the Advent story.

Christian discipline in the world calls for unclouded vision, unimpaired reflexes, and focused thought. *Let us be sober.*

Note that Paul does not say, "Let us be somber or sour." Too many Christians today look as if they were born with a mouth full of lemon juice. Nothing could be farther from the intent and spirit of this text. The Advent season is one of jubilation and great celebration. Yet, we are to be sober—as clear-headed, sharp, alert, and full-facultied as the grace of God allows.

Marked sobriety is the only faithful way to live through Advent—and any season of the Christian year.

Keep Awake!

Now, we look at the other imperative within this text: "Keep awake!" This command may have some of the meanings as does the order to be sober, but there is a varied pitch and new shade of interpretation.

Jesus told a number of parables about being "on watch." Likewise, the Old Testament is filled with "watchtower" images and reminders that those in the towers were to keep awake. The book of Proverbs has constant warnings against sloth among the people of God. The word *sloth* carries its own essence just in the sound of the word. Christian, in John Bunyan's classic *Pilgrim's Progress,* had to encounter and master Sloth on his journey toward the heavenly kingdom. We all do battle with sluggishness and sloth at times.

Here is the call to mental and spiritual alertness. It is critical to the journey for each disciple. We are frequently too much like the couple sitting by the fireplace one night. Both are slouched in their chairs, listless and lazy. After a while, the wife looks up and says to her husband, "Jed, I think it's raining outside. Why don't you go outside and check." And Jed says, "Oh, Ma, why don't you just whistle in the dog and see if he's wet!"

The clear call is to listen, to watch, to stay tuned, and to focus.

Remember your grade-school teacher who was always concerned about posture? I can still hear the constant prodding: "Sit up straight! Feet on the floor! Back against your chair! Chin up!" What was that all about? In addition to trying to set good lifetime habits, those teachers were well aware of an important truth: To maintain good posture is to be more alert and awake. In this text, Paul is aware of exactly the same thing as were my elementary teachers!

We must stay tuned. Occasionally, when our grandchildren are with us (or we are with them), I get preoccupied with something else. I will be reading or watching TV or engaging in a conversation. Off to one side, one of the boys will be calling constantly, "Papa! Papa! Papa!" And once in a while, either their mother or my wife will need to bring me to attention. "Brian, Andrew is calling you!"

Paul is doing something like that here. "Stay alert to what is going on," he insists.

Such alertness is especially important because it is not easy to discern all that is happening around us. Do we know how to read the world, or even our own lives, today? Do we know what kind of time it really is? I heard a marvelous lecture by a retired theologian. I shall never forget the words with which he began his lecture: "My friends, there are good days, and there are bad days. And this is certainly one of them."

Jesus says so often, "Watch!" To his disciples who fall asleep while he prays in Gethsemane, he says, "So, could you not stay awake with me one hour?" (Matt. 26:40). Again, he enjoins, "Get up and pray that you may not come into the time of trial" (Luke 22:46).

A Specific Instance

This brings a specific matter to the forefront of our thinking during Advent. There is a terrible battle going on around us during these days. It begins early in November each year (sometimes even earlier), and is relentless until the end of the season. It is the battle for the soul of every man, woman, and child. It is a battle for loyalty and attention. I see it everywhere, never more so than right now. And it is fairly brutal in its intensity.

It is the battle between the sacred and the secular. The secular says: "Buy! Spend! Borrow whatever you need! Go into debt! Just make sure that you make everyone around you happy!" The sacred says, more quietly, but fervently: "This is the season of the Word become flesh. This Word came and dwelt among us. It is a Word full of grace and truth. Unto us a child is born, a son is given. And his name is to be called Wonderful!"

It is a veritable tug-of-war. The battle may be the classic one between good and evil, between God and Satan. Or it may actually be more diversionary than sinister. Do we really know? I enjoy the cartoon that shows a minister in an informal gathering, responding to a question that has just been asked by a young woman: "Of course, I'm opposed to sin. I just don't know what qualifies any more." We don't really know how deep and binding this battle is.

We are in a stupor as we are pulled onto the wrong track time and time again. It is a dangerous state of apathy. I see it happening to myself more times than I care to admit. I see it happening to my grandchildren at a very tender age as well.

C. S. Lewis's classic *Screwtape Letters* is written as letters of advice from a senior devil (Screwtape) to his young nephew (Wormwood), a junior devil, on how to win a person over to Satan's kingdom. "Primarily," Screwtape advises, "we must distract the human beings. We must take away their attentiveness."

Paul cries out, "Wait! Don't you see what's happening?"

Our text, then, is a call to be fully alert!

If you happen to belong to a Covenant Discipleship Group or spiritual support group, Advent is the time *not* to miss a weekly session. If you are committed to reading Scripture and having private prayer at least once each day, Advent is the season *not* to miss even one day. If you occasionally attend the Wednesday evening prayer or healing service, Advent is the time *not* to miss any Wednesday evenings. Instead, Advent is the season to be sure that you worship weekly unless you are truly prevented. By the grace of God, there can be no slack in these days if we are to maintain a semblance of faithfulness in this annual struggle.

This is the month when we come to a "red alert," very much like military preparedness. Many Christians are uncomfortable with military imagery in the faith. Some were unhappy with the decisions to include hymns like "Onward, Christian Soldiers" or "The Battle Hymn of the Republic" or "Soldiers of Christ, Arise" in the new *United Methodist Hymnal*. But reason and good sense have prevailed. The military images are appropriate here. Paul is training troops for discipleship. We are training troops in the legacy of that same great tradition.

Don't let the secular drag you down into an empty pit of despondency and frustration at the end of December. Stay sober. Stay awake. Stay alert. Stay tuned in. Stay focused. Then, celebrate the season with a kind of spiritual gusto!

Journey Gently!

[Let us] be kind to one another, tenderhearted, forgiving one another, as God in Christ has forgiven you. (EPH. 4:32)

Over twelve years ago—while all of our children were still at home—we seized the opportunity for one of those extended family vacations we had dreamed about for years. We flew to Denver, Colorado, rented a motor home, and toured the great national parks of the West. It was a memorable family event.

Because one of my minor hobbies is photography, it was imperative that we take many pictures. We had a small problem, however: How could we make sure that the pictures taken would be identified with the correct park when the trip was completed? The family came up with a great idea.

Each park had a huge stone and wooden sign at the entrance gate: Zion Canyon National Park, Bryce Canyon National Park, Mesa Verde National Park, Grand Teton National Park, and so on. As we arrived for the first time at each new park, I would pull the camper off to the side of the road, and all four children would pile out and onto the park sign. After jockeying for position and space, they would cheerfully pose for a picture, and the slides would then be in appropriate order until the next such picture. It was great fun.

The process, however, actually made us all more aware of

other signs inside the parks. Signs pointed toward hiking trails. Signs warned us not to feed the bears. Signs indicated the height or depth of a particular trail to the base of a waterfall so we could estimate our stamina for making the trip. One sign, however, stands out in my mind. It was a small, carefully lettered sign just inside Yellowstone Park in Wyoming. It read simply, "Drive Gently."

> Be kind to one another, tenderhearted, forgiving one another, as God in Christ has forgiven you. (Eph. 4:32)

Here is another of the gracious imperatives for our discipleship—but one that is eminently suited to the Advent season. This is, after all, supposed to be a gentle season.

It was a gentle young woman to whom the angel came to announce the coming of Jesus. It was in a gentle way that this young woman and her betrothed husband, Joseph, made their way from Nazareth to Bethlehem—he alongside the donkey, she riding. The stable of Bethlehem was a gentle setting, one in which "Gentle Mary laid her child, lowly in a manger" (Joseph S. Cook). And the scene of the visit of the shepherds has always been—at least in the mind's eye—a gentle setting.

Here is a gentle text for a gentle season about life's call to journey gently.

Be Kind!

The text begins with the call to be kind. Kindness is a basic human quality. Jesus said, "Blessed are the merciful" (Matt. 5:7). The words mean, "Blessed are those who show and do kindness." The beatitude goes on to say, "for they will receive mercy." They will receive kindness performed toward them. In other words, kindness reproduces itself as one of the highest qualities of life. Kindness creates kindness creates kindness creates kindness!

The world observes a special feast during Advent. December

sixth is the day commemorated by many as the feast of Saint Nicholas. This marvelous human being was a bishop in Asia during the third century A.D. He is remembered as a man who spent most of his life doing kindness toward others without any thought of reward in return. He was especially kind to children. In so many ways, he lived a life imitative of Jesus. How sad that we have twisted and distorted and downgraded his image into that of Santa Claus in our own day.

Simple kindness from the heart is a great need—and a gracious imperative.

Sally Ernst, president of the Women's Division, United Methodist General Board of Global Ministries, wrote an article for *Response* magazine in November of 1989. Her words were in the form of a devotional meditation for Advent:

> I watched a little boy and his mother walking through the toy department of a large store. The child pushed toward the large display. He was excited as he talked to his mother. Finally, in exasperation he said to her, ''I have to have that. Everybody in my room has one. I need it.''

Sally then asked, ''What is it children need for Christmas? Even more important, what is it children really need to become whole persons?'' She then offered these words as a beginning of an answer: ''Children need persons—parents, grandparents, teachers, caregivers—who love them, nurture them, protect them from harm and provide for their needs.''[1]

Children need to see and experience kindness in order to develop as God's people. Kindness reproduces itself from generation to generation. ''Be kind to one another,'' Paul enjoins us.

Be Tenderhearted!

Next, he counsels us to be tenderhearted. This is not a condition of weakness but of strength. We tend to be more enamored of toughmindedness than of tenderheartedness.

Have you not met some persons who seem to find their very identity in being gruff and tough in the normal course of life? Paul says, "Be tenderhearted, gentle, peaceful." Such a disposition is more powerful than a loud voice or any title of authority.

Advent is the season to call forth tenderness. The Pittsburgh Peace Institute has these thoughtful words as part of their mission statement: "Nonviolent strategies can empower just and desirable social change." Do you believe that? I do. Gentleness of spirit can empower just and desirable social change.

Advent is the season to be tenderhearted, gentle, peaceful. It is a time in our world to show forth a life-style that is tenderhearted, gentle, peaceful.

Be Forgiving!

Then Paul calls us to be forgiving. The forgiving life-style is one that is spiritually healthy and whole. To live forgiveness is to live a whole life in the kingdom.

Yet, we are prone to resentment. We are prone to carrying grudges. And *dis*ease results.

We are now reasonably certain that resentment is not only spiritually destructive, but physically and emotionally destructive as well. A fairly large percentage of all illnesses—chronic and other types—are due to the long-term resentments we carry in our hearts. Disease of mind and body is caused by our inability or unwillingness to forgive. This is precisely why the text for today is so important to us. This is why the text is indeed an imperative.

We have two adult children who have moved back home with us for a while. (Someone calls these children "boomerang" children—an apt description.) Fortunately, our experience has been a positive one in almost every way.

However, when our younger son returned, he brought not

only all his earthly possessions, but also a sixty-pound Labrador Retriever puppy. The dog's name is Buster—Buster Brown, the Wonder Hound, to be precise. I marvel at this dog, for Buster is essentially a forgiving creature. I can yell at him, scold him, swat him, and leave him alone in the house for hours when all of us are away from home; and when I return he comes to me, wagging his tail as if saying, "It's okay. I forgive you." It is a winning way. Buster just forgives and forgives and forgives. And he is a very healthy dog!

Forgiveness is an utterly healthy human life-style—for body, mind, and spirit.

The Foundation for Forgiveness

The primary motivation for forgiveness and its gentle style comes from God's forgiveness. Forgive one another, as God in Christ has forgiven you. We are essentially a forgiven people. The grace of forgiveness is abundantly at work in our lives.

Note that Paul does not say, "Forgive, and you *will be* forgiven." He does not say, "Forgive *in order to know* forgiveness." He says, "Forgive, as God has already forgiven you." Grace is at work simply by our faith that it is so. I am forgiven without condition, just because I believe and trust God for that great act. Forgiveness flows from God, through us, into the world.

A clergy friend of mine tells the story of a nine-year-old Filipino girl who claimed she talked to Jesus every week. The people of her village became aware of her special conversations, and they sought her out regularly for inspiration and advice.

Gradually, the fame of this little girl spread beyond her village and reached the ears of the Roman Catholic cardinal in Manila. He invited her to come to the city for an interview. She came under his directive and arrangements.

As she sat in his office, he asked her the obvious questions: "Is it true that you talk to Jesus regularly?"

"Yes, your eminence, it's true," she answered.

"And does Jesus talk to you?" She acknowledged that this was also true. The cardinal was concerned, and he wanted to take some precautions against the child's claims getting out of hand. So he provided her with a challenge and a test. "Would you do something for me?" he asked. She nodded assent. "Next week, when you talk to Jesus, ask him what sins I confessed at my confession this week. Will you do that?"

The girl agreed and returned to her village. The next week, she returned at the instruction of her religious leader. "Well, did you talk to Jesus this week?" he asked.

"Yes, your eminence, I did."

"And did you ask him what I confessed at confession this week?"

"Yes, sir, I asked him," she answered.

Thinking the matter would now be finished, he asked the final question. "And what did Jesus say?"

"Well, your eminence, he got the strangest expression on his face. He looked down and scratched his head. Then he said, 'You know, I don't remember. I don't know. I guess I've already forgotten.' "

The grace of forgiveness is extended even before we think to ask! "Forgive . . . as God in Christ has already forgiven you!"

Journey gently! Be kind. Be tenderhearted. Forgive!

On the desk of the senior administrative secretary in the office next to mine is a hand-lettered sign that reads, "Be gentle." It is a consistent daily reminder of a way of life.

Dr. Ormal Miller was serving the First Methodist Church of Topeka, Kansas, when he died unexpectedly at the age of 48 in 1948. He wrote "A Christmas Creed," which speaks to all of us at Christmastime.

> I believe that Christmas is a spirit, and they that find it must seek it in spirit and in truth. I believe that it is not a season of the year, but a way to live. It comes whenever wise men and shepherds bow down to worship at the same shrine; whenever

charity displaces intolerance; whenever old enemies forgive one another; whenever kindliness takes the place of ill will. I believe in the Christmas hope as the way to life for all persons and all nations. I believe that peace on earth and good will among all can become living realities in this generation.[2]

Journey gently! There is no other way to live fully, completely, holistically. Be kind to one another. Be tender-hearted. Forgive one another. Forgive, as God in the amazing wonder of grace has already forgiven you.

Here is a truly gracious imperative for this sacred season, and for all the seasons of our lives.

BRING LIGHT!

Let us then lay aside the works of darkness and put on the armor of light.   (ROM. 13:12)

Lights are surely a wonderful part of the Christmas season. Many persons choose to outline the shape of their homes in lights during these days of December. Some prefer to place a single light in each window, creating the sense of a warm candle glow against the long dark winter nights. Lights are the first ornaments placed on the Christmas tree each year.

It is estimated that in excess of 1.3 million people drive through a large public park in Wheeling, West Virginia, during the Christmas season to see the annual "Festival of Lights"—sometimes enduring four- and five-hour traffic jams to do so.

In our home in suburban Pittsburgh, the word *joy,* outlined in lights, has been for at least fifteen years the most dominant exterior decoration we offer for this season.

Lights are a part of the season. And that is good. It is very good.

Long ago, very near the beginning of time, God said, "Let there be light." And there was light. And God saw that the light was good (Gen. 1:3-4). But over centuries of time, humankind began to prefer darkness to light. God tried to break through the darkness (through the judges, prophets, and other leaders of Israel), but only partially succeeded. Darkness once again crept over the face of the earth.

Thus in the fullness of God's time—at the right moment and in the right place—God said once again, "Let there be light," and Jesus was born. Jesus brought a light that outshines all darkness (John 1:5). Christmas is about a light that no darkness can extinguish or erase.

In our text, Paul says, "Let us lay aside the works of darkness and put on the armor of light." Such a statement seems to put the coming of Jesus in the form of a gracious imperative. "Let us . . . " is an invitation, not a demand. It is gracious, not absolute. Let us put aside the darkness. Let us put on the armor of light.

Where do we connect with this imperative? Two possibilities toward which to move are (1) we must get to know the light and (2) we must be a part of the light.

Get to Know the Light

First, we must become acquainted with the Light. To sustain an intimate relationship with the One who is the Light is of the highest priority. We must get in touch with the Light.

The story is told of a small church in a rural area that was continuing to worship in a fellowship hall below ground level during a building program—where the room allowed for little natural light. (The sanctuary would be built on this foundation at some future time.) The hall for worship was often dark and murky when the people gathered. The pastor of this little congregation decided it would be nice to buy a chandelier for the room. He announced his hope to the congregation and called a special meeting for a vote.

When the congregation came together, he told them he desired their vote on whether to spend money for a new chandelier for the worship space, and asked if there was any discussion on the matter. One old farmer stood up and said, "Yes, indeed! I want to discuss it! I am against this purchase.

And I am against it for three reasons. First, no one knows how to spell the thing; so we couldn't possibly order it. Second, if we did get one, no one could play it. And last, what we really need around here is more light!''

What we really need in our lives is a knowledge of and relationship with the Light.

Newsweek magazine had a fascinating cover story on religion in the fall of 1990. Entitling the article ''A Time to Seek'' the writers of the story recognized something that sociologists of religion have known for some time. Large numbers of baby boomers in America are now in the throes of a midlife evaluation. The high spending of the eighties and the beginnings of the ''fast track'' nineties are fostering an identifiable emptiness.

The darkness wants to overtake us one more time. We are on a pilgrimage to connect or reconnect with the light. Sometimes that pilgrimage is obscure; sometimes it is obvious. But it is highly present for many Americans.

We need light to live fully. Medical researchers are now reporting the fact that we need sunlight to stay healthy. Apparently, the sun is required to develop a certain chemical in the brain. All of us thrive on some level of solar energy! When the sun does not shine for long periods of time, some people suffer from listlessness or depression. They struggle when the days are overcast for extended periods of time. The short days of winter are particularly fearsome for these people.

Some of us need sunshine to thrive on this earth. *All* of us need the Light of Jesus Christ to maintain overall health on the journey.

We must do all that we can to stay in the direct beam of the Light. The *Newsweek* writers said, ''Spiritual development takes time, discipline and hard work.''[1] That's a remarkable statement from the secular press. But it is precisely on target. If the church or the individual Christian trivializes the discipline required in this effort, we are gradually overtaken by the ever-lurking and encroaching darkness.

Sometimes the darkness comes slowly and rather imperceptibly. For almost ten years, nativity creches have been disallowed on the steps of government buildings or in public parks. Sacred concerts are no longer acceptable in public schools. (The real tragedy is the watering down of what was once "sacred." In many concerts today, "Jesu, Joy of Man's Desiring" and "Frosty, the Snowman" are sung in sequence on the same program!) Now, more recently, even the Christmas tree and the Menorah have come under fire as seasonal religious symbols.

We may not know exactly when or how it happens, but the darkness comes. It creeps into life. It infiltrates our daily walk. We are caught unaware, unless we are able to maintain the discipline of a relationship with the Light.

Personally, I need a few minutes to rekindle that relationship every day. It need be only a few minutes, but the time must be there. Occasionally, I need a few hours. Now and then, I need even longer—a few days or a week. If I don't take the time, I pay a price. The time, discipline, and effort are essential.

We must get to know the Light. "Lay aside the works of darkness and put on the armor of light."

Be a Part of the Light!

But we must also be a part of that Light. In the words of the title of this message, we must ourselves *bring light*. It is not adequate to simply know the light. We must also wear it. "Put on the armor of light!" says Paul.

One of our hymns says it rather well:

> Soldiers of Christ arise,
> And put your armor on. . . .
> From strength to strength go on,
> Wrestle and fight and pray,
> Tread all the powers of darkness down
> And win the well-fought day.
>
> (CHARLES WESLEY)

38

To be a light in the world against the darkness is our call. And there is so much darkness.

A family, on vacation, was touring the Carlsbad Caverns in southeastern New Mexico. The mother, father, nine-year-old son, and five-year-old daughter were in a large tour group in one of the huge "rooms" deep within the cave. The guide, after explaining the various formations inside the cave, announced that he would turn out the lights for a few moments so that the group could experience total darkness. The lights went out, and the room was black. After a few seconds, the five-year-old reached nervously for her older brother's hand. The boy was heard to say softly, "Don't worry. There is someone here who knows how to turn on the lights."

The world is asking—corporately and personally—if there is anyone out there who knows where the lights are. We are the ones who know, we who are the people of God.

When the storm clouds of war seem to be gathering in any part of the world, Christians must be bearers of the light of peace. "Blessed are the peacemakers," said Jesus, "for they will be called children of God" (Matt. 5:9).

When the tide of greed seems to invade all of life, and not just the business part, Christians are the ones who cry out, "Blessed are those who are found sharing, feeding, housing, clothing, visiting" (see Matt. 25).

The world looks for light where the darkness seems to be invasive and pervasive. We are the bearers of that light.

Storm clouds gather in our personal lives as well. So many souls are groping in darkness right now. Perhaps you sense the darkness overtaking you or someone you love. You are reaching for the light. The darkness can be fearsome and incredible! Death comes in unexpected places—a searing tragedy that cuts across life without warning or announcement, and we are plunged into darkness. Separation and divorce come, but they always seem to happen to someone else, never to us. And life is plunged into darkness. We have desperate times with our children (including our adult children) that seem to last for weeks or months or years. And those long days are dark. Similar to winter days in the far northern hemisphere, they are days of endless night.

The Christian community is the bearer of the Light. We have been touched by the Light, and now we carry it. We proclaim the Light that outshines all darkness.

A friend of mine belongs to a service club in his city. He told me that a speaker from the Air Force was demonstrating a special pair of goggles to the group one evening. He told—in somewhat technical language—how these goggles helped military personnel "see" in the dark. After the meeting, a few of those present (including my friend) were allowed to join the speaker in a dark room to try on the goggles. My friend said that the results were astounding. In this totally black room he could see the other persons, the pictures on the wall, and the other objects in the room. Something in those goggles picked up and concentrated the unseen light in the room so he could see.

What a marvelous parable for the church. There is some light in all darkness. We are the power that is able to pick up the beacon of unseen Light and enable the world to behold it more clearly. We are here to announce, to proclaim, to shout the message from the hilltops. We know and trust a God who calls us out of darkness into his marvelous Light.

Space scientists have long posited a theory about "black holes" in space. Black holes are dark cavities in which there appears to be no light whatsoever. The theory says that the force of gravity is so powerful that even the photons of light collapse in upon themselves under the pull. All light is gone.

The Christmas season is one in which to boldly proclaim that the Light of Jesus Christ can outshine even the black holes of space! There is a beacon of light against any and all darkness. Darkness does not have the last word. The Light has come. The Light shines in the deepest darkness. And the Darkness cannot, will not, has not overcome it.

Let us, then, by the grace of God, lay aside the works of darkness and put on the armor of Light.

GRASP HOPE!

Let us hold fast to the confession of our hope without wavering, for he who has promised is faithful. (HEB. 10:23)

The first sermon I ever preached was on the theme of hope. It was in 1960 while I was a senior in college. I had recently declared my intentions for the ministry. The sermon was preached in a little country church somewhere in eastern Pennsylvania. I have forgotten the town, but I can see that sanctuary as if it were yesterday. The congregation was rural in life-style, and many of them came dressed for the labors of that particular day.

I feel quite sure that the sermon was awful! I recall that it was filled with philosophical fragments regarding proofs for the existence of God. As such, it reflected my current position on a journey of faith, but it was woefully unconnected to that congregation's needs.

The text, however, was wonderful—and it still is! "Always be ready to make your defense to anyone who demands from you an accounting for the hope that is in you" (I Pet. 3:15).

Over the thirty years since that day, I have probably spoken several dozen times on the topic of hope. And if I ever preach a "last" sermon it will probably be on the theme of hope.

Hope is a precious commodity. Sometimes it is elusive and partly hidden. But hope is always a faith possibility. The text for this chapter, then, is in the form of a challenge: Reach out and take hold of hope! Seize hope! Grasp hope! "Let us hold fast to the confession of our hope without wavering. . . . "

Grasp hope! Another of the gracious imperatives for the fullest expression of discipleship in our time!

The Quintessential Message

Christmas is the quintessential message of hope. The *Random House Dictionary* defines *quintessential* as "the pure and concentrated essence of a substance." Secondarily, it is defined as "the most perfect embodiment of something." Both definitions are pertinent. Christmas is the pure, concentrated essence and the perfect embodiment of hope.

I know a man who, during the Advent season, signs all of his mail—instead of "very truly yours" or "sincerely yours"—with "Christmas is the best news yet!" A young pastor signs his correspondence year round with the words, "Hope and confidence."

Frequently, the fourth candle of an Advent wreath is the candle of hope. Appropriately, it is the candle lighted on the day closest to Christmas Eve. In the Christ Child is the perfect embodiment of hope.

Christmas Gives Sustenance to Hope

Christmas gives sustenance to the hope that is in us. Philosophers have said for centuries that each human being has within a reservoir of hope. "Hope springs eternal" indeed! We are not without human resources to sustain hope within and around ourselves.

Albert Camus, a French existential philosopher of this century, once wrote: "In the midst of winter, I finally learned that there was in me an invincible summer." To a very real extent, Camus is correct. There is a hope created in every human breast. We are creatures of hope.

A colleague of mine in the ministry tells the story of a man who was struck by a car while walking on a busy interstate highway. He was thrown several yards by the impact, and landed in some shrubbery a few feet from the side of the road. Badly injured, he could not signal for help. He lay by the side of the busy interstate for four days and nights, while hundreds of cars whizzed by. Only gradually was he able to crawl toward a place along the road where he was spotted by a passing motorist. He subsequently was taken to the hospital and was expected to make a full recovery.

We might be prone to criticize the negligence or preoccupation of all the people in the cars that passed by this man for four days. What impressed my friend—and what impresses me—about this story, however, is that the victim affirmed life so much that he hung on with great tenacity. He was determined to hold on to hope.[1] There is an extraordinary capacity to sustain hope within each human being. There is a reservoir of hope within each of us.

But human resources and human energy for nurturing hope eventually run dry. F. Scott Fitzgerald wrote, ''I began to realize that for two years of my life I had been drawing on resources that I did not possess, that I had been mortgaging myself physically and spiritually up to the hilt.'' Do you reach the limit on your credit cards each year? Do you exhaust the borrowing power of your home mortgage? Are you mortgaged to the absolute maximum? The Christmas season sustains, nourishes, and grows the hope that is beyond human capacities.

Some helpful insights along these lines are found in the Christmas message of the Gospel of John. John writes differently from Matthew and Luke, who are more narrative in style. John uses word images with great effectiveness and power. In part of his story, he writes: ''From his fullness we have all received, grace upon grace'' (John 1:16). John is proclaiming that the fullness of God is inexhaustible. We can never use it up completely. There is such an abundance of God that grace and hope are present in a limitless supply. The credit line of God's fullness is never depleted. The cup always overflows!

On a night long ago, God walked down the stairs of heaven with a tiny child in his arms. That child is the sustaining power of hope in human life. The writer of our text says, "Grasp that hope! Seize it! Take hold of it!"

We Are to Offer That Hope

The task of the church—and of every Christian disciple—is to offer the Christmas hope to a highly mortgaged world. We proclaim the hope that is God's gift to life. Having received and internalized the message of hope, we pass it on with energy and skill.

Dr. Bernie Seigel tells the story of a woman who was doing battle with cancer. The treatments were not going well, because her cancer was not responding. Reluctantly, her doctor told her that there was simply nothing more he could do. He was sorry, but she would just have to let the cancer run its course. She should begin to get her personal affairs in order.

Not willing to give up, the woman sought treatment in another country, using a method that was highly experimental and unlicensed in the United States. After a few weeks, she seemed to be responding quite well. She began to feel better and returned to playing the piano—one of the great enjoyments of her life.

When she returned to the United States, she made an appointment to see her doctor. She told him that she was feeling better and was even playing the piano again. When she informed him of her trip outside the United States to seek experimental treatment, her doctor became angry. He scolded the woman for making that decision, and he told her that there was absolutely no way the drug could work. Her presumed improvement was only an illusion. He was disappointed in her behavior.

The woman left the doctor's office dejected and despondent. The spark of hope disappeared from her eyes. She was hurt and confused. She went home, got into bed, and died that night.[2]

Our call is to offer hope with enthusiasm and confidence. Here is the gracious imperative in this text. Here is the assignment. We are to offer hope without wavering. We are a sign of hope in the world.

Even our presence in a service of worship may be a sign to some. Those who drive by your church may see a full parking lot, or even recognize your particular car, and begin to ask themselves certain questions. Maybe there is more to life than I realized! Maybe there *is* a purpose after all! Maybe I do have reason to hope.

A theology of hope is a contagious theology. Years ago, a noted German theologian published a book on the theology of hope. It caused quite a stir in theological circles. It was a fresh entry into the dialogue. Hope is real. Christmas is that great good news.

I know a young couple who now live on an Army base with their children. Recently, the wife wrote me of her disillusionment regarding the religious life on the base. She and her husband teach Sunday school to a very small group of children. Chapel worship on the base is attended by fifteen to twenty persons. Chaplains are in short supply, and are not always available for the Sunday services. She was discouraged.

In my reply note to her, I said, "Remember that you are a sign of hope. Hold on to that hope tenaciously!"

Large crowds of people attend worship on Christmas Eve. Why do they all go? Some go because of pressure from family members. Grandma is in town, and she says, "Okay, everybody, it is Christmas Eve, and we're going to church!"

Some go because it is a habit to do so. They are like the little boy who was asked by his Sunday school teacher why he believed in God. He replied, "I guess it just runs in the family."

Some people come to church on Christmas Eve because it runs in the family.

But many come—I am quite convinced after a quarter century of observation—because the church is a sign of hope in their lives and in the world.

The gracious imperative is this: Be a sign of hope in a fragmented world. Hold fast without wavering. That is a large part of what it means to be a disciple this Christmas season.

One day, very close to Christmas, a child was coming down the hall at church on the last day of a special weekday Bible school. He had in his hand a little ceramic tray that he had made for his mother. As he ran down the hall, he tripped and fell. The tray broke into several pieces. The child was devastated. He began to cry loudly and uncontrollably.

People tried to comfort him with all kinds of counsel: "It was just a tray." "You can make another one." "It was nothing." "You can give your mother something else." The child was inconsolable.

Finally, his mother arrived on the scene. She immediately realized what had happened. Bending down beside her son and his broken gift, she said, "Well, now, let's pick up the pieces and take it all home. We'll put it together and see what we can make of it."

Isn't that exactly what the Christmas message is about? The world is broken into many fragments, as are our lives. God stoops down beside us. "Well, now," he says. "Let me help you pick up the pieces. We'll put it back together and see what we can make of it."

Men and women! Youth! Boys and girls! Let us hold fast to the confession of our hope without wavering, for he who promises is steadfastly faithful.

WOULD YOU LIKE TO HOLD THE BABY?

For a child has been born for us. . . .   (ISA. 9:6)

Among the most memorable experiences of my life have been the births of our children. I was privileged to be present in the delivery rooms when all three were born. I fully understand that such a practice is commonplace today, but it was *not* so twenty-six years ago when our oldest was born. I was the first father ever to be present in the delivery room at Morristown General Hospital in 1964. And I was the first father to make such a request of the obstetrician who delivered our son.

Both the hospital and the doctor were anxious about our request. As a result, I was *very* carefully prepared for the occasion: a sterilized gown, a sterilized cap on my head, a mask over my face, and careful washing of my hands before entering the delivery room. In addition, however, I had to sign a form that absolved the hospital of any liability if I should faint. In essence, the form said that the hospital would treat my wife and the baby as a first priority and tend to me afterward!

Our son was born about 9:30 on a Saturday morning. (All male preachers' children are born on Saturday to make the wives nervous about their Sunday morning loyalties!) Within a few minutes of birth, a nurse was standing in front of me with a very special invitation: "Dad, would you like to hold the baby?"

I think I had prepared myself for just about everything *except* that moment. Such a possibility had simply not occurred to me. What should I do? Would I make a mistake? I knew that I had only one choice, and that was to respond with a yes. I nervously held out my arms, and she handed him to me. It was a moment not to be forgotten. He was wrapped tightly in a receiving blanket, and I remembered something about the meaning of "swaddling clothes" in the Bible's nativity story.

This past summer, our third grandchild was born. I arrived at the hospital about two hours after delivery and entered my daughter's room with great anticipation. This time, there was no sterilized gown, no mask, and no head piece. And there were no papers to sign. This time, it was my radiantly smiling daughter who said, "Dad, would you like to hold the baby?"

Frequently, when I visit a couple from my congregation who have just had a new baby, I am given the same opportunity. "Would you like to hold the baby?" I never turn down the opportunity. Each new moment is special.

Do you suppose that Mary offered this same opportunity to the shepherds on that night in Bethlehem long ago? Do you suppose she said to them, "Would any of you like to hold the baby?"

The shepherds had arrived at the stable excited and breathless. They had moved quickly up the hillside from their fields to the place where Jesus was born. They were both frightened and excited by what had happened. The sky had split apart earlier that evening with the singing of angels. The music was still ringing in their ears. Without any thought about who would care for their flocks, they had come to town. Not one of them had stayed behind. They had found the inn, and then the stable behind the inn. Quietly, very unsure of what they might find, they had entered this simple place. And there, before them in quiet lantern glow, was a new family. There, lying in a manger (a cattle feeding trough) on a bed of fresh hay, was the newborn child.

Can you see Mary studying the shepherds for a few minutes? Can you see her examining their faces one by one? Do you suppose she could see in their eyes that they had experienced a vision from God? Did she intuitively understand that the shepherds had been told what she and Joseph had been told earlier? And then, can you hear her ask, with growing trust and openness, "Would any of you like to hold the baby?"

How do you suppose they might have responded? What would the shepherds have done with that invitation? I don't know, of course. But I would like to imagine what happened. And I can imagine myself—and some of you—in their response.

I suspect that a couple of the shepherds are so preoccupied with what they see that they never hear her offer. One shepherd, for example, is just plain dumbfounded. "This can't be the right place," he thinks. "This is not the kind of setting that angels would sing about! The angels talked about the coming of the Savior of the world. This can't be the right place. Maybe we have come to the wrong family. The wrong stable. The wrong baby." This shepherd simply cannot get past the incongruity of the situation. So he never hears the offer to hold the baby.

Another shepherd is caught up in a different kind of thought process. He wants to believe, but he just can't. All his life, he has wanted to believe that God would send the promised Messiah. But this is not the way the Messiah will come! He has heard the stories of the promises from his family before him. And he has heard the message of the angels. But he is stuck with his doubts and misgivings. Sure, he would like to believe that this child is the Savior of the world. He wants to believe that God is in this setting. But he can't make the leap of faith. At least not yet. And his wrestling with this stumbling block makes him unable to hear the special invitation from Mary, "Would you like to hold the baby?"

Another shepherd hears the invitation very well, and he responds with absolute certainty. "No way! Not me! I don't do babies! I can't hold anything that tiny, that fragile, that new. I wouldn't know what to do!'' He's too uncomfortable with infants. He's happy to leave babies to mothers—like Mary. He says out loud, ''I'll look. I might even touch. But I won't hold. No sir. Not me.''

One shepherd, however, is eager to respond to the invitation. ''I would like to hold him,'' he says quickly and with excitement. He is Reuben. A bit older than the others, he is a father himself—and a grandfather.

At the invitation, he reaches down and gently picks up the newborn child. The child is awake, but does not make a sound. Reuben holds him slightly away from his body so that they can look into each other's eyes. He gazes at the child, and the child gazes back. The stable is reverently silent.

Reuben thinks about many things: What special gifts will this child bring? What will life be like for him? What will it mean that he is the ''Savior of the world?'' How will he be *my* Savior? Reuben puzzles over many different kinds of questions out into the future.

Mary looks at him, a bit curious. ''What are you thinking?'' she asks.

''Oh, nothing,'' he replies. He's too awkward about sharing his innermost thoughts and feelings at this point. He's generally a very private person.

Reuben turns the baby into the crook of his arm. He's more relaxed now. He breaks the silence with some banter about babies in general, about the crowds in Bethlehem, and about the weather. The initial spell of quietness is broken somewhat, and the entire group breaks into animated conversation. There is baby talk and laughter.

In the midst of it all, Reuben feels a tugging at his tunic. He looks down and—he had almost forgotten—sees his six-year-old grandson. Benjamin had been with them in the field that night. He had to race hard to keep up with the men when they left for Bethlehem, but he had come with them. He wanted to see this baby about which the angels had sung.

"Grandpa," the child says, "can I hold the baby?"

Reuben is not quite sure how to respond. He glances over at Mary, who smiles and nods approval. "All right, son. Sit down over there." He points to a pile of straw. The boy is seated, and his grandfather lays the child in his arms. The boy beams with pride.

Benjamin looks at Jesus much as his grandfather had done. All eyes are fixed on the child holding the child. There is silence once more. Benjamin asks a question: "Grandpa, is this the baby about which the angels sang?"

"Yes, Benjamin, this is the child."

"Then, Grandpa, this is the One who is to be our Savior?"

"Yes, Benjamin, I believe he is the One."

Finally, there is a curious and somewhat unexpected question: "Then, Grandpa, am I supposed to love Jesus?"

Reuben puzzles for a moment, and then says, "Yes, Benjamin, you are to love him."

With that, Benjamin suddenly takes the baby and pulls him close to his chest—very tightly. The whole assembly gasps as one! They are concerned that the boy might hold the baby too closely and injure him in some way.

But the baby is fine. There is no sound or sign of discomfort. And in the quiet, all hear little Benjamin say boldly and with his whole heart, "I love you, baby Jesus."

Benjamin lowers the baby from his special embrace and hands him back to his mother. Mary is smiling, through a flood of tears.

Can you see all of this? Do you see what I see? Hear what I hear?

Would you like to hold the baby? Can you imagine your response to the invitation for just a moment? Can you see yourself in that stable of Bethlehem with this child in your arms?

What do you see in his eyes? Can you see in him the light of life? Can you see the great hope of all humankind? Can you see the promise of peace on earth? Can you see in him the very meaning of your existence? (He is, you know! He is the meaning of your life and mine!)

Can you see in this tiny child the promises of wholeness and of eternity?

Would you like to hold the baby?

Maintain vision!

Only let us hold fast to what we have attained.　　(PHIL. 3:16)

Many people are content to hold on to things as they are in life. The words of our text for today are from Paul in Philippians: "Only let us hold fast to what we have attained." Some might assume that this text is a call to that very status quo—to maintain the existing state of things.

I suppose there is some value in that, and some justification for such a reading of the apostle. At the beginning of one new year, I spoke with a member of my congregation who was reflecting with me upon some pending decisions for the coming months. The decisions were in regard to certain ministries that might be beyond the financial means of our church. She said, "Brian, we simply can't lose hold of anything right now. We need to hold on to everything we now have in place."

In some regards, this could be deemed an appropriate stance. The text is a kind of celebration of the status quo.

If you are a member of a church in which there is some small growth in membership and participation, you might authentically say, "We are growing a bit. Let's just hold on to what we have right now. Let's not change things too much."

If your church has a steady number of small groups for Bible study or faith sharing, you could say, "We are doing all right. Let's just stabilize where we are right now."

If your church is trying to listen to the hurts and needs of the community around you, and you have one or two missional ministries in place, you could say, "Let's make sure that these thrusts are strong and secure before we try anything new."

If you happen to have an active, vital youth group in your church and some good adult advisers, you could say, "Let's make sure we take care of these kids. Let's not stretch ourselves too far and risk losing what we already have."

More Than Status Quo

But there is more to the power of this text than holding on to the status quo. There is more to affirm here than what is happening now. What is the larger picture? What is the more comprehensive meaning behind Paul's imperative? What is the undergirding theme that led us to a particular positive point? What has allowed us to progress in our own discipleship or in the mission of our congregations?

The answer is *vision*. We are a people of vision. Christ's people are a people of vision. We have been given the ability to see deeply into the fabric of life. We live creatively on the edge of the great adventure. We are never satisfied with what is. We always hold up the vision.

What is the concept or power that allowed us to become who we are? To realize what we have attained? The answer is "vision."

Therefore, hold fast to the vision of a new order of things. Hold fast to the hope of the kingdom on earth as it is in heaven. Hold fast to the vision of an authentic, radical discipleship. The gracious imperative this day and this new year is: Maintain vision!

The people of the Old Testament period had numerous prophets through their sacred history. Prophets were not those who could foretell the future. Rather, they were those who could see the hand of God at work in the present, and thereby call God's people into a new future. The prophets were those who issued the divine call of God for obedience, for justice, and for righteousness.

One of the prophets said it quite succinctly: "Your young people shall see visions, and your older people shall dream dreams" (see Joel 2:28). In many ways, this text is a call to a new prophetic ministry into the twenty-first century.

Clearly, not everyone is a visionary in our time. I acknowledge the fact that "visioning" is not my own special strength. But I surround myself with persons who are visionaries, because I believe visioning is the call and claim upon the Christian community in our day.

The call to vision is our call as followers of our Lord. It is a fully gracious imperative. We must trust the vision of some. We must listen to the wild dreamers who speak from time to time. Recall the words of the wisdom writer in Proverbs: "Where there is no vision, the people perish" (29:18 KJV).

One of America's great hockey players was asked how he could score so many goals in any given game. How did he know how to find the puck and slam it into the net time and time again? His reply was simple: "I try to anticipate where the puck is going next instead of seeing where it has been."

Christians try to anticipate where the signals of God are moving and where they are headed next.

The story is told of a fisherman who was casting his line from a dock one day. A few yards away was another man who was also doing some fishing. The first man noticed something curious about the other fisherman: He was throwing a lot of the fish he caught back into the lake. Furthermore, he seemed to be keeping the smaller fish and throwing back the larger ones.

Finally, the first man's curiosity got the better of him. He walked up to the man and asked what he was doing. The man said, "I have a ruler in my hand. If the fish I catch is ten inches or less, I keep it. If it is longer than ten inches, I throw it back."

"But that's crazy," the other replied. "Why don't you keep the larger fish?"

"Because," came the answer, "I only have a ten-inch skillet."

Followers of Jesus Christ cannot be people who are limited by a ten-inch skillet!

Called to Be a People of Vision

Disciples in the twenty-first century (and even those of this final decade of the twentieth century) will need to be visionary. This is true for clergy, employed lay staff, and lay leaders of our churches as well as for every individual disciple. We shall stay tuned to the promptings of God. We will ask the questions, "What if we risked this direction?" or "What would happen if we tried this?" We shall proclaim and be attentive to sensible visions as well as to visions that are—at least on the surface—quite preposterous.

David Lowes Watson was asked how to know when something is a "prompting" of God. His reply was clear. We test that prompting in a gathered group of God's faithful people. We ask one another to reflect upon it prayerfully. Is this a vision of God? Or is it something of lesser value?[1] Thus we continue to be constantly exploring God's visions through our individual lives and in our lives together.

Herb Miller's book *The Vital Congregation* appeared in mid-1990. The first chapter has an intriguing title: "Your Most Important Employee." Since I have a fair number of people employed in my congregation, I hurriedly read the chapter to find out who is most important. His definitive answer is that the most important person or persons in your church are those "lay and clergy leaders who model and communicate a vision of hope and expectancy regarding the future."[2]

Each of us is under that call of God! The most important member of the board of trustees is the person who has vision. The most important member of the choir is the one who has vision. The most valuable teacher in the Sunday school is the one who has vision.

Carl Sandburg once said, ''Nothing happens without first, a dream.'' So it is in the life of faith.

Don Shelby, senior minister of the First United Methodist Church of Santa Monica, California, once spoke these words in a sermon:

> We need a purpose large enough to include God and long enough to include eternity. We need a purpose that makes life worth living, and that gives meaning to our dying so that we can exit this world with imagination and laughter. We need a purpose for life that calls forth our true stature and elicits the hidden fire within us and sustains our commitment to the end. We are called to exist with imagination and courage, because we have a purpose that lasts past sundown.

What About Resources?

Some will inevitably ask, ''What about resources? Will there be enough money for these visions? Will there be enough human talent? Will there be enough time?'' Those who are anticipating the dilemmas for the church of the next decade suggest that time will be the most precious and sought after commodity. It will be of the nature of human beings—including many Christians—to hold on to time more closely than they have ever held on to money.

Dag Hammarskjöld once wrote, ''We live in a world where our resources are only limited by our vision.'' Such a statement must be especially true of the followers of Jesus Christ.

In the Christian journey, the resources are given by way of spiritual gifts. There are many spiritual gifts among God's people.

There are gifts of justice and compassion. Perhaps you have that gift. You call your family and loved ones as well as the body of Christ toward greater expressions of justice and compassion.

There are gifts of peacemaking. Perhaps you have discerned God's clear call to be a peacemaker on behalf of the whole community of faith. Your vision is that of peace. Your dream is for a peaceful conclusion to each and every conflict. You call others into action toward this end. You know both the call and the promise of Jesus' words, "Blessed are the peacemakers, for they will be called children of God" (Matt. 5:9).

Perhaps you have the gift of giving. A man said to me long ago, "For some reason, I have been given the gift of making money. I want to be sure that I use that gift as responsibly as I can."

Perhaps you have the gift of teaching. You have a vision of children or youth or adults who are better equipped and informed disciples.

Perhaps you have the gift of caring. You envision a large or small Christian community of people who care deeply and effectively for one another. You feel keenly the pain and hurt that afflict life so frequently.

Do we have the resources for the vision? Remember these words of Paul: "[God] by the power at work within us is able to accomplish abundantly far more than all we can ask or imagine" (Eph. 3:20).

Are you concerned about human resources? Consider this statement regarding John Wesley's England in the eighteenth century:

> The Methodist's purpose of spiritual seriousness and holy living left an abiding stamp on both church and nation. Methodists never numbered more than a fraction of one percent of England's population during Wesley's lifetime; but their devotion and commitment was the talk of the land.[3]

There are resources to match any and every vision that is of God. There is, therefore, no reason not to hold fast to that vision.

Evangelist Tony Campolo writes about the time he flew into Hawaii to speak at a conference. His bout with jet lag was terrible. He could not sleep, and he was hungry. He found himself up at 2:00 A.M., walking the streets around his hotel, looking for a place to get something to eat.

Finally, he found a diner that was open, one of those places we might call a "greasy spoon." He sat down at the counter and ordered a sandwich. A few minutes later, a small group of women, who were obviously prostitutes, walked into the diner. They sat down at a nearby table and ordered coffee. Campolo heard one of them say, "Tomorrow is my birthday. I'll be thirty-seven."

"Big deal!" said another. "So what do you want me to do about it?"

A while later the group left the diner. Campolo turned to the cook and asked, "Do those ladies come in here every night?" He was assured that they did, at almost exactly the same 2:00 A.M. hour. "Do you suppose we could arrange a birthday party for that one woman tomorrow morning?" he asked.

The cook was sure they could, and the plans were set in motion. The cook's wife even baked a cake. News about the party went out on the street. The next night, at about 2:00 A.M., a small crowd had gathered in the diner. Right on schedule, the same three women arrived. The one who was having the birthday could scarcely believe her eyes. A party just for her! She was so moved, she could hardly muster the breath to blow out the candles on the cake.

Just before the party ended, Campolo walked over to the group and offered a prayer for them—for their well-being, for a new life in Christ and in faith for each one. Slowly, the diner emptied into the night.

When they were alone, the cook said to the evangelist, "I didn't know you were a preacher. What kind of a church do you belong to?"

"I belong to a church," came the response, "that loves

people and that throws birthday parties for prostitutes at 2:00 in the morning!''

"You know," the cook replied, "that's the kind of church I could join."[4]

Hold fast to the wild, incredible visions of God. Don't ever let those visions get away.

You know, that's the kind of church with vision.

Cultivate Compassion!

Let us be concerned for one another. (HEB. 10:24 GNB)

Have you ever felt "compassion fatigue"? That is, have you ever experienced being worn out from doing good? You consider yourself to be a generous, self-giving individual, a person who shares from the heart. But there are just too many needs, too many crises, too many appeals. And finally, you want to say, "Enough! Just go away!"

Somewhere, a vicious tornado strikes, and a town is devastated. The bishops issue an appeal for relief funds, meaning a special offering from your church. A refugee crisis in the Middle East requires the donation of blankets and temporary shelter. Someone solicits funding for the care of babies with AIDS in Rumania. A single parent in your community needs child care and meals while she recovers from major surgery. And a fire in another part of the city burns the home of a family of seven. No lives are lost, but there are urgent appeals for goods to replace the basic needs of this large family.

And, for a moment—at least for a while—it just seems to be too much. Compassion fatigue sets in.

There is some evidence that Jesus came close to compassion fatigue in his earthly journey. He needed to get away from the endless demands for healing from the restless crowds. He needed to renew his energies for the wants that pressed upon him. Jesus experienced human emotions.

Have you ever felt compassion fatigue? In the midst of this difficult and complex question comes another imperative for authentic discipleship: "Let us be concerned for one another, to help one another to show love and to do good" (Heb. 10:24 GNB).

Curiously, the New Revised Standard Version of the Bible renders these words a bit differently: "Let us consider how to provoke one another to love and good deeds."

I will let the Greek scholars debate the exact translation. However, the message is quite clear. We are to do all we can—by the grace of God—to respond to the needs and hurts and pain around us. Such a life-style is part of Christian discipleship.

Be on the Leading Edge

Such a call will have increasing urgency and higher priority in the coming years. We are called to be on the leading edge of compassion. We are to be initiators of the good. We are to be *pro*active, not simply *re*active. We are to seek ways to show mercy, to do kindness, to express love, and to spread compassion with full energy and intention. We are to assess our faithfulness in this regard on a daily basis.

We do not wait until the opportunities come our way. Instead, we seek the opportunities. We ask God to clear our agendas sufficiently so that we are attuned to the needs for compassionate responses around us. There is even evidence in the teaching of John Wesley, spiritual founder of The United Methodist Church, that deeds of mercy and compassion must be the first concern of every disciple. We are not to neglect the care of our own souls (prayer, devotional time with Scripture, the sacraments), but we are to make very certain that compassion is of the highest priority in our obedience under grace. Wesley seemed legitimately concerned that acts of mercy and compassion might be lost in the quest for personal piety.

God is calling us to new parameters of compassion, to new boundaries, to ever-expanding boundaries. We are to be resourceful, sensitive, and attuned to the ever-changing and often complex distress and poverty of our times. We are under a gracious imperative to enlarge and to enliven the presumed limits of compassion in our midst.

What are the arenas for this revitalized compassion?

Within the Household of Faith

One arena is certainly our own community of faith—the congregations to which we have formal or extended ties. Paul writes that we are to show love and compassion "especially for those of the family of faith" (Gal. 6:10). It may be only a beginning point, but it is vitally important.

Every church consultant I know says the same thing: The churches that will make a significant difference in the coming years are those that take seriously the quality of caring in their congregational life. Such congregational caring cannot be casual or accidental or loosely constructed. Compassionate works of mercy and love must be thoughtfully, carefully, and creatively initiated.

Over my ten years of ministry at my present church appointment, the number of clergy on staff has decreased at least three times. A reluctant vote of the board has sent us from five to four to three and one-half to three clergy—the latter being our present constellation. Such decreasing has been a movement toward new strength for the congregation in lay leadership and in caring for one another.

At present, one of the associate clergy bears the title Minister of Congregational Care. His sole function is to watch over and implement the caring ministries of this body of believers and our extended family.

He is not to do it all. Rather, he is to use imagination and vision as well as computer technology for quality congregational care. The task of the Minister of Congregational Care is to "provoke us to love and good works" toward one another. The decision we made three years ago to have only three ordained clergy on staff is bearing fruit. We are not perfect by any means, but we are growing in our effective response to this particular call to discipleship.

Into the Surrounding Community

Another arena is the community around us. Even though the community I live in is considered to be upper middle class, the human needs there are enormous. Many persons feel that those who live in suburbia "have arrived." At a deeply human level, this is simply not the case. Sometimes the needs are hard to discern. We are adept at putting on masks. Many of our needs are well hidden and difficult to ascertain.

I enjoy the story of the woman who saw a man lying in the curbside gutter one day. Filled with concern, she rushed over to the man and knelt beside him. He seemed to have a pulse, but did not appear to be breathing. Quickly, she rolled him over and began giving him mouth-to-mouth resuscitation. The man looked up at the woman and said, "Lady, I don't know what you are doing, but I just lay down here to clean out this storm sewer."

Sometimes we make mistakes. We are not sure in every instance. But the needs are present in every area of human habitation. A few hundred feet beyond the walls of any church sanctuary are many needs that call for the response of compassionate ministries. The call of Jesus Christ is to listen and then to take risks on the side of compassion.

A small child-care center opened in the building of my church in September of 1981. As the center has grown, we have discovered that it has become a significant "listening post" for the community. As we listen, we learn of needs that we might otherwise have passed by: agonizing struggles by separating and divorcing parents, lonely and stressful vigils by adult children with elderly parents in the home, a growing dilemma regarding the care of Alzheimer's victims, the problems of latch-key children, and the guilt felt by parents who are not home when their children arrive home from school each day. Because we have tried to listen, we now have an entity known as the Christ Church Community Caring Network with at least nine separate and growing components to respond with compassion in the name of Christ to human needs.

Yet any recitation of recent history is not enough. The growing crises of hunger, unemployment and underemployment, homelessness, substance abuse, and home care-giving (to name only a few) press upon the people of faith. The real questions are these: What needs of the human family around us are we being called to address? What are we equipped for and called toward in the next five months or five years? Where is God leading us, prodding us, provoking us?

Every new Christian, every local congregation, and every Sunday school class faces this essential discipleship question: Are we listening?

A friend of mine discovered the growing need for support and encouragement of cancer patients in his church and community. A few years ago, he began a cancer support group in his church—a place where information could be shared and where stories could be told; a place where celebration of victories and tears of remission reversals could be told; and a place where the providential care of God could be proclaimed and affirmed. It was a ministry of compassion that brought laughter and tears, healing and hope, and that created powerful ties of friendship among persons struggling against the similar powers of disease and death.

God clearly issues gracious imperatives for compassion now. God calls us to new arenas. Where will God's leading take you next? And me?

Might we be called to be advocates for an AIDS hospice in our community? Surely, this is a volatile, yet crucial, cutting-edge compassionate ministry! Is there too much compassion fatigue? Or can we respond with conviction? Listen to this statement from a recent writer:

> Could it be that AIDS, rather than being viewed as "punishment" from God for sin, is in some way a "word" from God—a call to his people to respond with compassion to those who might otherwise die without knowing they are loved? Will the church respond with hysteria and judgment [or with compassion]? [1]

Where will the Spirit of God lead us next? Do we believe that God gives the energy *and* the call in our time? Do we believe that God will not only *provoke* but also *provide* the means? I do!

The Larger Arena—the World!

And what about the even larger arena—the world? I recently saw an advertisement for an agency known as "Compassion International." I know nothing about the agency itself, but it is a good guiding phrase for the people of God.

What we do with our best gifts of love and money and kindness affects the whole world. A corn farmer won all the blue ribbons for his corn year after year at the county fair. Yet, each year, he shared his best seed corn with neighboring farmers. "How do you expect to continue winning blue ribbons if you give your best seed corn to others?" he was asked.

"You don't understand," said the farmer. "The wind carries the pollen from field to field. And if I am to have the best corn, I must see to it that all my neighbors also have the best corn. If they produce poor corn it will pollinate mine and pull my quality down."[2]

What would happen if we abandoned our endless (and fruitless) pursuit of being better off in favor of the pursuit of compassion? Listen to these choice words:

The world would be better off if people tried to become better. And people would become better if they stopped trying to be better off. For when everybody tries to be better off, nobody is better off. But when everybody tries to become better, everybody is better off.[3]

God calls us to channel our energies toward responding to the world with compassion. Compassion is closely linked to justice in the Scriptures. A portion of a well-known quotation from the Old Testament prophet Micah says it succinctly:

> What does the LORD
> require of you
> but to do justice, and to love
> kindness . . . ?
> (Micah 6:8)

God calls us to a solid commitment to compassionate justice.

Hearty compassion for the whole world is the way of Jesus. It is the way of discipleship. It is a gracious imperative. The significant retirement activities of former President Jimmy Carter have been well documented. In one of his insightful editorials, James Wall made this closing observation in *The Christian Century*: "These days Jimmy Carter no longer needs to worry about prominent scholars looking for ways to use his religion against him. Instead, he stays busy, travelling about doing good because his religion tells him he must."[4] Compassion is a way of life. It is the way of Jesus.

A tragic event took place in 1972: A terrible earthquake struck near Managua, Nicaragua. Immediately following the disaster, two dramatically different responses were made. One was made by an incredibly wealthy man, Howard Hughes, who left his hotel in Managua, picked his way through the rubble to his private plane, and flew out to a luxury hotel suite in Europe.

Another man, Roberto Clemente, beloved superstar right fielder of the Pittsburgh Pirates, chartered some cargo planes and began flying into the devastated area with medicine and emergency food supplies. On one of those trips, Clemente died when the plane went down in an accident in the open sea.

The question before us regarding compassion is simple: Are we flying out? Are we flying in? Or are we just flying by?

In the name of a merciful, gracious God, let us stir one another up. Let us provoke one another to love and good works. It is the clear and clarion call of Jesus Christ.

Focus INWARD!

Let us come near to God. (HEB. 10:22 GNB)

Most of us can look back on a year—or even a few months—and be assured that the time has been anything but dull. If your life is like mine, it has been filled to capacity, even overflowing, with busyness. That seems to be the way we live these days.

A portion of the stimulus for such multi-faceted lives comes from external sources. We may live in a city where there is a potential division-winning professional athletic team. Such possibilities can generate excitement and foster new kinds of time commitments. Contrast that with some world-shaking event that rivets our attention—the unexpected invasion of one nation of the world by another (such as Kuwait by Iraq in 1990) or the unexpected death of a major political figure, which drains off our vital energies in yet another direction. Add these two possibilities to an already full life, and our emotional systems quickly flash "overload."

For pastors, the life of a congregation can create hectic schedules for extended periods. In one recent year, my local church had an inordinate number of hospital stays for members—higher than at any time I can remember. At the same time, there was an extraordinary number of new births, baptisms, and weddings. Clergy staff, lay staff, and lay pastors were all scheduled to the limit at key times.

The pressure of multiple jobs for members of family households creates incredible schedule dilemmas. Recently, my wife maintained two part-time jobs for several months. In one particular week, she found herself scheduled for something almost every day and evening. As we parted on Monday morning, she said, "See you next weekend!" My mind raced through unexpected schedule complications, and my mouth—I am sure—was agape as she smiled and exited to the garage!

Add to all of this the triumphs and tragedies in personal and family circles, and you know that life has too often been very full. Each of our lives sustains a lot of emotional and spiritual ups and downs in any given period of time.

Through it all, however, the Christian pilgrim strives to remain faithful.

The most important call to discipleship is that of renewed, revitalized faithfulness. Such a call is not an oppressive legalism laid upon us, but an invitation under grace to explore that which gives life meaning in the midst of chaos. Where in the midst of chaos is "shape" to be found?

An appropriate text for consideration is from Hebrews 10:22: "Let us come near to God." Or, as it is sometimes rendered, "Let us draw near to God." Two messages surface within this gracious imperative for discipleship.

Centered Lives

First, our lives must be centered. This is surely a worthy way in which to observe the early days of any new year—by recognizing the need for centered lives. We get so easily off center—regularly or occasionally.

During a recent summer vacation, we spent some time with our daughter and her family as they moved into a newly built house in Chesapeake, Virginia. We did some papering, built some shelves, hung pictures and window blinds—that sort of thing. In preparation for all of this, I asked our daughter to ascertain from the builder what the distance was between the wall studs.

She reported that they were on 16-inch centers, the presumed standard of the industry. As I began my rather unskilled carpentry work, however, I discovered very quickly that the studs were not uniform. They were 15 inches or 15 1/2 inches or 17 inches or 16 1/2 inches. Only occasionally did I find them on evenly spaced 16-inch centers.

It is hard to maintain the focus of our Center in these days—and it is getting harder! Only at the center point are our lives sufficiently strong.

One day during that same visit in Chesapeake, our daughter came home with a new porch swing for me to install. The home has a 5-foot wide porch, and she bought a 4-foot swing. However, porch swings require some special handling in their installation. The huge screws must be located in the very center of the beams overhead. Otherwise, they may break loose and send the swing crashing down. (Since I was to know the privilege of a few delightful summer evenings on that swing with my new granddaughter in my arms, I had special reason to be careful and accurate!)

Only at the center does maximum strength occur.

A member of my congregation said to me recently, in the midst of some personal tragedy and through tears: "Brian, how do people make it without God at the center of their lives?" How indeed? This is a time to determine to stay on center with our lives.

During the 1960s, there was a play on Broadway about a black mother and her two adult children, living in a tenement apartment in Chicago. The play was entitled *A Raisin in the Sun*. In one memorable scene, the mother is confronted by her daughter's angry skepticism, when the daughter says: "Mama, you don't understand. It's all a matter of ideas, and God is one idea I just don't accept. . . . There is simply no blasted God—there is only man and it is *he* who makes miracles.''

I can still see that mother as she looks at her daughter with the quiet majesty of her spiritual integrity and says, ''Now—you say after me: In my mother's house there is still God.''

After a long pause, while the daughter realizes what her mother's faith has meant to the family down through the years, she says quietly and slowly, ''In my mother's house there is still God.''[1]

Several of my local church staff members have told me of an interesting and troubling dynamic at work in some of our family households over recent months—especially homes where there are children and youth.

It is becoming widely apparent across America that our children are as inundated with activities and schedule conflicts as adults seem to be. The situation has become especially heavy in recent years. Thus some parents are giving their children choices: ''What would *you* like to give up?'' And they are sometimes choosing to give up choir or youth group or weekend children's educational ministries at the church.

These are not good choices, and to give children these choices is not responsible parenting. Where is it written that ''good'' parents are the ones who allow their children to make their own decisions at every turn? Children hunger today for guidelines, a strong sense of priorities, and careful modeling.

In the midst of all the change and the competing claims of life, God is still most important. There is only one Center. It will require great fortitude of spirit—as persons and as parents—to affirm boldly exactly where our priorities lie. It is a gracious imperative: ''Draw near to God.''

Basking in God's Presence

The second point around this text has to do with the means by which to draw near to God. We need to do some basking in the presence of God each day.

I say this with some hesitation, for I know that some Christians think this is *all* that the Christian life is about. They take no risks of faith and discipleship for the kingdom in the world. I am not advocating such aloofness here. This is precisely why the preceding chapter (on cultivating compassion) encourages compassionate ministries as a first-order priority in our quest for authentic discipleship.

But we are also in need of basking, of soaking up the presence of God from time to time. We need to luxuriate in God on regular occasions.

We are geared to produce. Everything calls us to be productive, contributing, energetic, and prolific workers in the "vineyard." The old Protestant work ethic comes to the forefront of life. I know it well. I was raised and trained in that ethic.

But in order to stay on Center, we must place ourselves in the Presence of God. We must just *be* in that Presence on a regular basis.

One of the best things to happen to me in the church in the last five years is Covenant Discipleship. Modeled on the Wesley class meeting, Covenant Discipleship is a small group of persons who meet for one hour weekly to be accountable for some basic spiritual disciplines—daily prayer, reading of Scripture, regular worship, and participation in the sacrament. We also add specific objectives under our own covenant that we deem to be important to our growth—works of compassion and mercy, concerns for justice, and learning to listen to the promptings and warnings of God's Holy Spirit.[2] Sometimes, involvement in the covenant seems to imply that we are to be busy "doing"—reading the Scriptures, praying daily, worshiping, receiving communion, performing acts of mercy, taking care of minds and bodies, and so on. However, if we do not take the time to step into the Presence of God, we burn out and actually lose energy.

The hardest thing I have to do in my own daily devotional time is to just "be" in the Presence of God, quietly, for a few minutes. I am geared to accomplish, to produce, to get it done, to make it happen. My covenant group has meant more to me in this regard than has any other discipline in my entire Christian life.

I spoke with someone recently about the new Disciple Bible Study program now being used in hundreds of United Methodist churches across the country. Knowing the rigorous discipline that this study entails, I asked, "Isn't that also a 'work ethic' type of schedule—with heavy reading responsibilities, a certain deadline to meet, and homework requirements?"

"Yes," she answered, "but with an important qualification. There is a sabbath in each week—one day out of each seven. There is one day when the student is requested to lay all of the work aside and reflect, meditate, consider what God may be saying to us in the studies of the past week."

I read a sermon recently on the fourth Commandment: "Remember the sabbath day, and keep it holy. . . . The seventh day is a sabbath . . . you shall not do any work" (Exod. 20:8, 10). The message was cleverly but appropriately entitled, "Give It a Rest!" The sabbath was created to allow some basking in the presence of God.

There is much value in the receptive mode, in some contemplation. Before we can breathe out, we must breathe in.

A pastor once told the story of a man who was an avowed agnostic in his congregation. One day, this man's daughter—whom he truly idolized and loved deeply—became gravely ill. As he sat by her bedside—as she hung in the balance between life and death—he put his head in his hands and wept. He muttered aloud, "God is nowhere. God is nowhere."

In a few seconds, he felt his daughter's frail hand on his face and a finger wiped a tear from the corner of his eye. He heard her whispered voice saying, "Oh Daddy, you are so wrong. God is now here. God is now here!" When we know that God is now here, we are focused, ready, and able to meet life with creative discipleship.

These words follow shortly after the words of our text: "in

full assurance of faith," so that the imperative reads, "Draw near to God in the full assurance of faith."

Here is the quiet confidence that no power on earth can take away. This is what I want for you and for me. I pray for the great assurance of centered lives, and I pray for the fullest awareness of a God Who is now here!

When we have lived the fruits of this gracious imperative, the resultant faithfulness and vital discipleship will inevitably follow.

Worship Faithfully!

Let us not give up the habit of meeting together, as some are doing. Instead, let us encourage one another. (HEB. 10:25 GNB)

Thomas Carlyle, the nineteenth-century essayist, philosopher, and historian, once said, "No greater calamity can befall a nation than the loss of worship." His was a remarkable insight, and one that was highly prophetic.

The writer of Hebrews says something very similar in the text quoted above. Worship is absolutely essential to the vitality of a congregation and the journey of discipleship. It is the energizing center. It is the centerpiece on the banquet table of Christian experience.

Ten years ago, a well-known church consultant predicted that Christians would not be worshiping at 11:00 A.M. on Sunday mornings by 1990. He now testifies that the durability and resiliency of the local church is far greater than he had originally assumed. Sunday morning is still the dominant time for Christian worship.

Today, news analysts and consultants are predicting the demise of vital worship in American churches by the turn of the century. They conclude that there will always be a remnant—but only a remnant. They, too, will be amazed at the durability—and the necessity—of worship in the Christian pilgrimage.

Yet, there *is* a problem. We cannot simply assume that things will be as they have always been. The quiet, steady erosion of key disciplines in our lives can transform us into purely secular creatures almost without our noticing.

"No greater calamity can befall a nation than the loss of worship." "Let us not give up the habit of meeting together." Where do such words meet our own moment in history?

There is no serious question today about the competing claims against weekly worship times in our lives. It is true that 87 percent of Americans indicate that they have been in a worship service at some time in their lives, and 40 percent (less in the North and West, more in the South) tell us that they have been in a church or synagogue for worship in the last seven days. But competing claims keep wearing away some of the experience of worship.

Employment requirements at primary and secondary jobs place greater demands on us—especially for those in the newest sectors of the job market. Increasing numbers of us work more hours each week than we did a few years ago. Such schedules eat into the precious few discretionary hours we have in any given week.

Sports and extracurricular activities for children and youth are scheduled on Sunday morning or over whole weekends. Extra part-time employment for various family members means scattered and very full weekend schedules. All this results in fragmented families with little commonality of direction.

The gradual encroachment of the secular causes some of the most essential grounding of life to deteriorate. It is a quiet, persistent, destructive process—without necessarily being openly evil.

For many persons, worship becomes hurried at first. Then, it gravitates toward a reluctant option for one or more family members. Occasionally, and finally, worship is dispensed with altogether—almost without anyone realizing what has happened.

Right now, there is an extraordinarily high number of

persons in the United States who profess to believe in God and in Jesus Christ. But the number who sustain a weekly habit of worship in their lives is statistically shrinking.

Is worship a legalistic requirement? I used to think so. As a child—and even into young adulthood—I read the fourth commandment as a thundering rule of God: "Remember the sabbath day and keep it holy!"

I now believe that worship is in the category of a gracious imperative. It is a part of discipleship under grace. It is an encouraged act of faithfulness by a gracious God. Someone said recently, "Worship is not a legalistic requirement of an angry God, but a loving desire of a loving God who just wants to spend some quality time with us."

Why do we worship? What value does it have?

I suppose you have heard some of the statistics about where the largest percentage of accidents happen in this country. Twenty percent happen in the automobile. Seventeen percent happen in the home. Sixteen percent happen to persons walking or running—injured pedestrians. Fifteen percent happen in some form of conveyance other than the automobile. *But only .001 percent of all accidents happen in church!* Thus the safest place to be is in church.

Surely, there are better reasons for worshiping. I want to offer two.

Connecting with God

First, worship helps us connect with God. Herb Miller, in a fine book on the local congregation, recently wrote, "Churches do many things, but their main thing is helping people connect with God. Worship is the primary way churches accomplish that main thing."[1]

Somewhere else, I read: "The main thing is to keep the main thing the main thing." So it is with worship as a connecting event.

A woman was marveling at how quiet a certain teenager was

in the presence of company. The teen's mother replied, "Oh, she starts talking only when she hears a dial tone."

Worship is a matter of being connected to the dial tone of God's presence. Worship is like plugging in a power tool to the electrical source. Such connection does not guarantee that the tool will be used well, but it is connected.

A children's Sunday school class was asked, "Why do people go to church?" One boy responded, "My grandparents go to church every Sunday because they have known God longer!" Worship connects us with the Almighty on a consistent, continuing basis.

We deeply need to be connected. I recently saw a cartoon of a stereotypical scene in a psychiatrist's office. A woman was lying on a couch. The doctor was in his chair, full beard, notebook in hand. The woman was saying, "Doctor, I keep trying to get in touch with my deepest self, but all I get is her answering machine."

A friend of mine tells the story of a busy attorney who was racing through Chicago's O'Hare airport one Friday afternoon. The crowds were maddening, and he was trying his best to get to the boarding gate for his connecting flight. In the process, he came to a large crowd of children, all dressed in similar T-shirts. (He learned later they were from a Chicago children's home.) As he threaded his way through the children, he suddenly felt an arm around his leg.

He looked down to see a handsome blond-haired boy of about six staring up at him. "Who do you belong to, mister?" the child asked. "Can I go with you?"

The question haunted the attorney as he finally boarded the plane and took his seat. He later reported that the question ultimately became life-changing in its impact. "To whom *do* I belong?" he thought to himself. "To my profession? To my investments? To my clients? Or to the God who once was real to me?"

Worship connects us and reconnects us. It is strength and

power for living. It is a regular need in each of our lives.

I used to balk a bit at the old "filling station" image of Sunday worship services. It seemed to cheapen worship to say that it was simply like filling up at the pump. Now, I am not so sure that the image is inadequate.

Worship connects us to a Source of power and love. William Willimon wrote, "The foundation of a Christian view of ethics, or politics, or anything else begins in worship, in the sometimes dark, passionate, scary, fiery tempest of God and people colliding on Sunday."[2] We need that colliding and connecting. Let us never give up the habit.

A new FM radio station in my city has as its slogan: "Bright and Easy!" Most of us wish that life was like that—bright and easy. But we know it is not. Worship connects us with the power that we need in the times when life is anything but bright and easy.

Worship connects us with others who are also connected. One of my favorite sayings is from Dietrich Bonhoeffer's writings: "The physical presence of other Christians is a source of incomparable joy and strength to the believer."[3]

Someone else has powerfully written, "How special are the Lord's faithful people. My greatest pleasure is to be with them." Is not this writer recognizing the power of community worship for communing with God?

Worship is a connecting event. Therefore, let us not give up the habit of meeting together!

Pointing to Greater Possibilities

Second, worship points us to the greater possibilities in our lives. As such, worship is a kind of preliminary event. It is an overture to the larger picture. It is a hint of what can be.

Worship may be our "main thing." It may be a community event. But it is not the end in itself. Worship is not the totality of the Christian experience.

I often wonder whether a Sunday morning greeting, prior to a spoken call to worship, ought to sound something like this:

> Good morning
> It is wonderful to have you here.
> Listen for the possibilities.
> But don't mistake this experience for the whole thing.

Worship is our energizing center. But it is not the equivalent of discipleship. Because of worship, we want to know more.

Worship says, "There are boundless possibilities for life in Christ. We challenge you to find those possibilities. Listen for them. Make some connections. Then move on those connections. Come on board. Join a great procession."

There is a marvelous story of a brilliant young Soviet Communist Party member who had a conversion to Jesus Christ. The exact manner of his conversion is not told, but the excitement of the experience would not allow the man to keep silent. He knew that to speak of the experience would deny him both advanced education and advancement in the party itself.

In spite of this, he one day told of his newfound faith to another party member. His friend replied, "You must be realistic. These things you speak of are for your kingdom of God and it has not come yet."

And the young Christian replied, "Sir, I realize it has not come for you or for the Soviet Union or for the world. But the Kingdom of God has come for me!"[4]

Worship opens up the possibilities for the kingdom of God in our lives.

Hebrews 10:25, then, is a strong, gracious word of deep encouragement. "Don't lose your worship. Don't neglect the space in your lives for meeting together. Don't give up the habit."

In 1944, a well-known British preacher began his sermon on the BBC by saying that the world can be saved by one thing only: worship![5] Such words form a bold, strong statement. But it is still true, and it always will be.

Let us, then, not give up the habit of meeting together. Instead, let us encourage one another, for no greater calamity can befall us than the loss of worship in life's journey.

CHAPTER 11

PURSUE PERFECTION!

Therefore let us go on toward perfection.   (HEB. 6:1)

I had a good friend in my first congregation who had a great deal of difficulty with Jesus' call to perfection: "You must be perfect" (Matt. 5:48 GNB). And he used that text as an excuse not to make an absolute commitment to the Christian faith. He thought those words to be an irrational and impossible ideal.

Similarly, some new ordinands into the ministry of The United Methodist Church have difficulty with the questions that are asked of them at the time of their reception into full membership. One of the questions is this: "Do you expect to be made perfect in love in this life?" and another: "Are you earnestly striving after it?"[1] Do you wonder that a significant number of these men and women have been known to mumble their responses to such questions?

In spite of these two instances, I contend that one of the gracious imperatives of Christian discipleship for the twenty-first century is perfection. We should have a distinct passion for perfection.

We are assisted in our understanding of this imperative by the variance in translations of the Greek word rendered "perfection" or "perfect" in the New Testament. The actual meaning is that of being fully grown or mature. Thus *maturity* is an adequate synonym for *perfection*. This is brought home in Hebrews 6:1, quoted above.

Therefore, this gracious imperative is: Let us go on to maturity in the Christian life. It may be one of the most important calls to discipleship that we in the church shall ever hear! And, as always, it is enveloped in grace!

Maturing Should Be Enjoyable

Neill Hamilton, a distinguished theologian and teacher, asserts that maturity is the real fun of the Christian journey. And he is right! As important as conversion is, and as important as the new birth may be, the real joy is the ongoing path toward Christian maturity. An ever-growing maturity through the years of life as a person of faith is a source of deep satisfaction and joy.

A lot is made of John Wesley's Aldersgate experience in May of 1738 at "about a quarter before nine." Yet, even that experience was a transition for Wesley, not a conversion. It was a new beginning point, a new launching toward the enjoyment of what it means to be a Christian.

The great joy in life is that of growing, deepening, and broadening the spiritual life—and of watching that same event in the lives of others.

Joe Paterno has been the head football coach at Penn State since 1965. It is reported that a few years after joining the staff at Penn State he received a phone call from the management of an NFL franchise, asking him to consider the head coaching job with that team. Paterno rejected the offer, saying that he was very happy with his current position.

The caller then made Paterno a financial proposal that was stunning—well in excess of one million dollars, part ownership of the franchise, and a huge signing bonus. Paterno said that he was then earning $35,000 per year at Penn State. How could he refuse? He had to take the offer.

That night, he lay awake most of the night. He thought about his family and their home, which had been the only home they had ever known. He saw images of the granite mascot on the campus—the Nittany Lion. And he saw each of his "thick-necked, fragile-hearted" players, one by one. Why had he said he would leave? He knew the answer. It was the money. And he also knew that he had changed his mind.

The next morning, he told his wife, "You went to bed with a millionaire, but you woke up with me! I'm not going." Later, he wrote:

> I now know clearly, exactly, and forever just what college football means to me—and what professional football never could. . . . Pro football is about winning. Only winning. . . . Just winning is a silly reason to be serious about a game. . . .
>
> I love winning football games as much as any coach. My players love winning. . . . But we also draw on an underlying layer of strength and power that gives us an advantage. While committing everything we've got to playing our best game, we know there's something that counts far more than winning. . . .
>
> . . . I watch almost all of our players grow in the game, grow in their personal discipline, grow in their educational development, grow as human beings. . . . That is a big, deep lasting reward.[2]

There is a deep and lasting satisfaction in growing toward maturity in the Christian life, and in watching that same seasoning process in others.

The Church as Modeling Agency

An attractive body of believers (or even an individual Christian today) is one committed to the maturing process, one with a passion for maturity. A friend of mine serves a church located very near a small shopping plaza that has—as one of its storefronts—a modeling agency. One day, he walked from his office door to the parking lot to be confronted by a stranger, who asked, "Pardon me, but is this the door to the modeling agency?" He tried to think of a quick, witty response. He also felt somewhat flattered. But in the end, he simply directed the person to a door a few feet away.

Nevertheless, it is not a bad image. We hold up a likeness of what makes life worthwhile. We are not perfect in any traditional meaning of that word. But we point the world in the direction in which life ought to be headed. The essence of the Christian life, rightly understood, is highly contagious!

Some Definitions

What does *Christian maturity* mean? It means growing in the ways in which faith and life are integrated. It means growth in relation to the real connection between faith and life in the world. It means seeing God as directly related to all we are and all we do.

One of the great German preachers of the previous generation wrote these words:

> So there is nothing in my life that is not changed after I have learned to say, "I believe." When we have found God, not one stone is left upon another in our life . . . people we meet, landscapes through which we drive, streaks of bad luck and affliction, and the bright hours of our life when we feel as though we will burst with happiness and delight—there is nothing which is not seen in a new light when the joy of faith is given to us, and our whole life is calmed because we have found peace with God. It is no wonder, then, that all of us yearn for faith.[3]

Many of you will remember the Dave Dravecky story. Dravecky was a professional baseball player. On August 10, 1989, he returned to the mound for the San Francisco Giants after having radical surgery to remove a malignant tumor from the bone and half of a major muscle in his pitching arm. His doctors had predicted that his pitching career was ended, but he proved them wrong. On that night, he pitched and won a game against Cincinnati. It was a magnificent performance for any pitcher.

In a post-game press conference, Dravecky said, "Before we go any further, I want to say that I give all praise to Jesus Christ. Without Him, there is no story."

Four days later, while he was pitching another game, the arm broke again. The strain on the bone without the whole muscle was too much.

When reporters cornered Dravecky again, he once again offered his praise to God. When they asked him about his pitching career, he told them that he had placed his future in God's hands.

A certain Bay Area sports columnist took exception to Dravecky's religious witness. In his column, he wrote:

> To make a public spectacle of religious feelings only cheapens them. Dave Dravecky is shortchanging himself when he gives God credit for his comeback. God didn't lift those weights and endure those excruciating exercises. God didn't overcome the fear that a career might be over. Dravecky did!

Dave Dravecky replied to the columnist with this simple statement: "Certainly God did not lift those weights for me, but God did give me the courage and the perspective to deal with adversity—and even with heartbreak."[4]

Christian maturity is the radical improvement of our perspective. It is seeing more and more of life as being provided by God's grace and good news—even in times of adversity. Maturity is a goal and a gracious imperative for the Christian journey.

An Uncomfortable Truth

However, an uncomfortable truth has become more apparent in our day. Christian maturity is *weakening* in many mainline

Protestant congregations. The passion for maturity—even a little bit of it—is not of much real concern to many of us.

The Gallup Poll has recently released some new data about American religious preferences in 1990. The data shows that a record number of Americans now profess a commitment to Jesus Christ. Three out of four say they have such commitment—74 percent to be exact. But nowhere does that poll suggest that we are moving anywhere with that commitment.[5]

Early in 1990, the results of a three-and-one-half-year study funded by the Lilly Endowment were released. The study analyzed the presence of Christian maturity in Protestant adults. More than 11,000 persons were interviewed in 561 local congregations.

The results were these: Only 32 percent of all Protestant adults have an integrated (maturing) faith. Thirty-six percent have an undeveloped faith. The remainder have an underdeveloped or underdeveloping faith. Thus *most* church members have not made Christian maturity (moving on toward perfection) a priority in their lives.[6]

What Is the Solution? The Cure?

Where then do we grow that maturity? Where do we get back on track with the ripening process in the Christian life? Where do we learn to integrate our faith?

The Lilly Endowment study says that *Christian education is the most vital factor in this effort.* Christian education has twice the impact of any other force in the local church. Worship connects us with God. Christian education facilitates growth.

In my local congregation, we struggle mightily—and against some cultural forces—to build an adult Sunday school and an adult education program. The tide of the times works against us, but we keep the pressure in place.

The Lilly Study says this:

> Effective Christian education is the most powerful single influence congregations have on maturity of faith. Researchers also claim that Christian education has the potential to renew congregational life and reverse downward membership trends.[7]

Some of you have undoubtedly said to yourselves, "Is Sunday school really important at my age? Isn't the Disciple Study or some other biblically based adult study for those who have made a more radical commitment?

The answer seems clearer than it has ever been: To learn in a setting with others is to ensure some growth. Since growth is the only evidence of "life," the call and claim of God is clear. Maturation is a gracious imperative for effective discipleship in our time.

About a year ago, I began teaching an adult Sunday school class at a rather early hour on Sunday morning—before any worship services began. Such a decision represents, in part, my own understanding of the differences between worship and Christian education. *Both* are absolutely essential. Worship connects us. Education helps us move on to perfection, to maturity.

This is why we have Bible study each week in our adult day-care center (for people who are elderly). And I am told that the Bible study hour is the point in the week when the largest number of clients are registered.

This is why we have Bible songs and Bible stories in our child-care center. With care and sensitivity, we have a passion for maturity at every level of the Christian life.

It Will Make a Difference

Such passion will make a difference, and it will bear good fruit. Recently, I came across a short quotation from Albert Outler, the man who was often known as "Mr. Methodism."

These are the closing words of his last public lecture, and offer a final challenge to you and me: "Hold fast to Christ; and as for the rest, hang loose, while doing all you can to honor His Name and the Christian cause."[8]

Hear again the call of Jesus: "You must be perfect." You must be a maturing disciple.

Hear again the challenge to new clergy: "Expect to be made perfect in this life!" Expect to be a maturing Christian throughout life.

Hear again the text—a word to each pilgrim: "Let us go on toward perfection." Let us, indeed!

C H A P T E R 1 2

Spread Encouragement!

Therefore [let us] encourage one another and build up each other, as indeed you are doing. (I THESS. 5:11)

A wonderful story tells of two cowboys out on the range caring for a large herd of buffalo. One of the cowboys says to the other, "These buffalo are the dirtiest, smelliest, ugliest creatures on the face of the earth."

Hearing this statement, one nearby buffalo turns to another and says, "I thought out here we weren't supposed to hear a discouraging word!"

Discouragement is so easily spoken these days. Encouragement is hard to find in many quarters.

Encouragement is far too easily omitted in the daily business of life. I read of a very wealthy man who took great pride in never tipping anyone for service. One day, this man suffered the tragic loss of his chief personal accountant through suicide. At first, it was assumed that the accountant was guilty of some creative bookkeeping. But this was not the case. A note said simply, "In thirty years I have never had one word of encouragement. I'm fed up!"[1]

Encouragement is difficult to find in the institution of marriage. We neglect to affirm and build up each other in marriage covenants.

A marvelous story tells of a husband and wife. One night when they were in bed, the wife thought she heard a burglar downstairs. She nudged her husband and said, "I think I hear a burglar, and he is in the casserole I made for dinner tonight."

The husband replied, "Oh, let him alone. I'll bury him in the morning!"

Marriage needs encouragement in abundance these days. Every time I sit with an engaged couple in preparation for marriage, I ask each of them a very pointed and deliberate question: "What kinds of encouragement will _____ need from you during the first five years of your marriage?" The question often causes a long, penetrating silence. But I always wait for an answer.

I sit with an individual in a complex life situation, or with one who has just been terminated from twenty years of faithful employment. I pray and search for words of encouragement. What does it mean to offer hope in the light of the text that says, "We know that all things work together for good for those who love God" (Rom. 8:28)?

Encouragement is hard to find in our time. Encouragement, it seems, is actually a specialty. It is the specialty of the people of God. We are to spread encouragement throughout the land.

Jesus frequently told parables to encourage his small band of disciples, for they became discouraged on a number of occasions. One of my favorite parables is that of the "seed growing secretly."

> The kingdom of God is as if someone would scatter seed on the ground, and would sleep and rise night and day, and the seed would sprout and grow, he does not know how. (Mark 4:26-27)

Clearly, this is an instance of giving encouragement to the disciples. Can you hear the conversation in the inner circle? The disciples ask, "Lord, are we ever going to see any results? Will what we have done here really make a difference? Is any of this going anywhere? Is anything really happening?"

And Jesus answers, "My dear friends, let me tell you a parable. Consider the seed that grows secretly. The farmer plants it. The seed grows. But the farmer does not know how it happens." In other words: Take heart! The future is securely in God's hands.

As a gospel writer, Mark sought to encourage Christians in the face of rampant persecution. Luke, in a somewhat different style, sought to give encouragement in the light of the presumed delay in the Second Coming of Christ. Encouragement is a dominant theme of both Gospels. In a real sense, Mark and Luke are theologians of encouragement.

Paul addresses the same theme in several of his Epistles:

Be mutually encouraged by each other's faith. (Rom. 1:12)
Speak to other people for their upbuilding and encouragement
   and consolation. (I Cor. 14:3)
I want their hearts to be encouraged. (Col. 2:2)
Encourage the faint hearted. (I Thess. 5:14)

Finally, of course, the text for this message: "Therefore [let us] encourage one another and build up each other" (I Thess. 5:11).

To spread encouragement is one more of the gracious imperatives of accountable discipleship. Spread encouragement throughout the land.

What are the arenas of our encouragement—both as a received gift and as a matter of witness?

Encouraged, As to the World

In many circles, Christians are presumed to be pessimists regarding the future of creation. Messages with regard to time—and especially end time—always seem to have an ominous ring. To prepare for the coming of Christ in our lives too often implies to prepare for the end of all life and all time.

Perhaps you have heard this limerick:

God's plan made a hopeful beginning;
But we spoiled our chances by sinning.
  We trust that the story
  Will end in God's glory,
But at present, the other side's winning!

The early messages about the Persian Gulf crisis in August of 1990 brought the prophets of doom out of hiding one more time. This time, it was not only the Christians, but also some Jewish sects that saw signs of the end. In ancient rabbinic literature there are writings that tell of the war between the Persian king and the Arab king. Additionally, according to these writings, other nations do not know what side they are actually supporting. In the midst of such confusion and turmoil, the Messiah will come, and the world as we know it will come to an end. Most of us are familiar with similar prophecies from the Christian tradition.

What does all of this mean? If the world is about to end, then the world must not be a very important place to God! Is the whole divine purpose of history to end history?

I don't believe that! I don't believe that God wants the world to come to an end. (Please note that if the world does come to an end—by some tragic error or miscalculation or by the armed uprising of greed—I deeply believe that God will be there at the end. I just do not believe the end is near in God's scheme of things!)

God loves this world, even in the fallen state of creation. This is at least part of the focus in John 3:16: "God so loved the world. . . ."

Recently, I read these words of Louis Evely:

> I often say to myself that, in our religion, God must feel very much alone; for is there anyone besides God who believes in the salvation of the world? God seeks among us sons and daughters who resemble God enough, who love the world enough that God could send them into the world to save it.[2]

We are to spread encouragement regarding the continuance of time and this marvelous, though troubled, creation.

Encouraged, As to the Church

So many people with words of gloom and doom for the church are out on the streets these days. Pessimists abound with claims regarding the future and the viability of the local congregation as a significant entity for the foreseeable future.

The Apostle Paul helps me immeasurably on this point to see that every church has a purpose. Every church has certain gifts. Every church has a calling, a task to perform. Not all churches are alike. Some are very large, some very small. Some are rural, others urban, others suburban, and still others are small-town. Not all churches have the same gifts. The important matter is to discover the gifts and to put them to work for the kingdom.

I read about a chicken yard into which a football was accidentally kicked one day by some children playing nearby. The old rooster walked over and took a long look at the football. Then he summoned all of the hens to one corner of the yard, stood on a rock, and pointed to the football. ''I want you to see what some of the hens in other places are doing!''

Churches are not in competition with each other. We must not covet one another's gifts. The church is called by God for ministry and mission in each community. We need not be marginalized by popular opinion or by critical theologians. We are a creation of God.

Not long ago, the bishops of The United Methodist Church released an important pastoral letter and document to the church. They presented a ''vision'' for the church. Here are a few crucial sentences from that pastoral letter.

We the bishops of the church declare our commitment to congregational vitality and faithful discipleship. . . . We believe that the central expression of ministry and mission in

Christ's name is the local congregation. Here, the gospel is preached and taught. . . . Here discipleship finds its source and its direction. . . . We the bishops of the church yearn for a vital congregation in every place. . . . As bishops we commit ourselves to lead our annual conferences in discerning God's vision for the church and congregational life.[3]

Here are some of the most encouraging words ever to come from the bishops of The United Methodist Church. They speak to us of promise and hope, of possibility and direction in congregational life into the twenty-first century.

Let us encourage one another and build each other up.

Encouraged, As to Life

God's love is showered upon each life in this world. Your life is valued. My life is valued. Such affirmations need to be deeply implanted in each mind and heart and soul.

A prominent physician was visiting a bush mission hospital in a Third World country. As he walked through the facility, his attention was drawn to a particular nurse who seemed to excel in her work—a professional knowledge of medicine, a kind and caring manner with patients, and an easy rapport with co-workers. After watching her carefully for a while, the doctor called her over. "I have been watching you," he said, "and I can see that you are an excellent nurse. How much do they pay you here?"

The nurse told him the amount. "My dear," the doctor replied, "that is not nearly enough."

"I make enough to live," she responded.

"But you deserve so much more, at least fifty or seventy-five dollars more per week. God knows you are worth it!"

A quiet, confident smile came over the nurse's face. She placed her hand on the doctor's and said, "Well, doctor, if God knows I'm worth it, that's all that really matters, isn't it?"

Spread encouragement! Each of us is of incredible worth to God. Every life is precious.

A father and his daughter were on a cruise ship together after the untimely death of the wife and mother. As they stood on the deck of the ship one day, the little girl looked at her father and asked, "Daddy, does God love us as much as Mommy did?"

The father thought for a moment and then said, "Honey, God's love reaches farther than you can see in that direction." He pointed to the far horizon. Then, pointing in the opposite direction, he added, "And God's love reaches farther than you can see in this other direction." He pointed up toward the sky. "God's love is higher than the sky." Finally, he pointed down over the rail of the ship. "God's love is deeper than the ocean."

"Oh, and just think, Daddy," the daughter replied, "we're right here in the middle of it all!"

So it is. We are surrounded, loved, and kept in the gracious heart of God. Our lives are precious to God in every way.

Encouraged, As to Faith

A major brokerage house and investment firm has claimed for years that they are "bullish on America." I am bullish on faith! Faith is a solid bet for the journey of life.

I suppose my greatest personal growth over the years of my ministry has come from my being increasingly persuaded of this singular truth. Every attempt to tear at the fabric of my faith has been mended by the grace of God. Every attempt to trivialize faith has led to a deeper profundity. Every attack on belief from logic or science or some other intellectual discipline has led to a surer and more certain hope in my mind and heart.

It is worth everything in life to put ourselves into a faith picture—to risk the leap of faith with our talents, with our financial resources, with our time, and with our family. We can assuredly risk all we have to invest ourselves in faith in Jesus Christ.

Spread the word: Faith in Jesus Christ is a solid bet.

We are encouraged; therefore, we spread encouragement. We are agents of encouragement for our world.

Such a stance is not "Pollyanna" thinking. Neither is it a cheap form of positive thinking. The stance comes from a deep, abiding trust in the Lord of history.

In a small church in Leicestershire, England, there is a plaque in memory of the founder of that church. It reads as follows:

> In the year 1653, when all things throughout the land were either demolished or profaned, Sir Robert Shirley, Baronet, founded this church, whose singular praise it is to have done the best things in the worst of times, and hoped them in the most calamitous times.

That's it! That's the gracious imperative for discipleship. It is, perhaps, the most imperative of the "imperatives" for the immediate future.

We are to do the best things in the worst of times, and to hope the best things in the most calamitous of times. We are to spread encouragement throughout the land.

Sustain Spirituality!

If we live by the Spirit, let us also be guided by the Spirit.
(GAL. 5:25)

A Sunday school teacher had assigned each member of her class some research on a particular portion of Christian dogma. The following Sunday, she called for the report on the Holy Spirit. There was a prolonged silence, until finally one little girl raised her hand and said, ''Teacher, the boy who believes in the Holy Spirit is absent today.''

For a long time, that statement has been true of many of us in the church. The Holy Spirit has been marginal to our faith. We knew or thought little about the matter.

I grew up without much conscious awareness of the Holy Spirit in my life. True, I sang the doxology each Sunday in worship: ''Praise Father, Son, and Holy Ghost.'' And I sang the Gloria Patri on a regular basis: ''Glory be to the Father and to the Son and to the Holy Ghost.'' However, I gave little thought to what the Holy Ghost meant.

How many times at summer camp did I sing, reverently and with feeling: ''Spirit of the living God, fall afresh on me''? But I never really considered the power of that prayer.

I once heard a masterful lecture on the Holy Spirit by the eminent theologian Karl Barth in the chapel of Princeton

University. In his broken English and with profound serious-ness, he said, "You American Christians have difficulty with the Holy Spirit because you refer only to the Holy Ghost. It sounds too much like a 'spook.' " As he spoke those words, I knew he was probably right.

Still, the Holy Spirit was not a major factor in my life. Then came the decade of the 1970s. The Holy Spirit came front and center for American theology. We had the rapid rise of the Charismatic Movement. Conferences on the Holy Spirit sprouted up all over the land. The Full Gospel Movement became a dominant Christian gathering in many communities. Faith was challenged. Unless one was "baptized in the Holy Spirit," he or she was not a full Christian.

Even a few friends of mine began to contest the legitimacy of my faith. I (along with others) began to reexamine what I believed. The end result was to reestablish a workable theology of the Holy Spirit.

Part of my early difficulty stemmed from the fact that I had not been given much help in the seminary I attended. The theology of the Holy Spirit was cursorily referred to as "pneumatology." I quickly—and, I think, understandably— put that topic on the shelf with phenomenology, ontology, epistemology, cosmology, and other seemingly irrelevant "ologies" of academia.

But no more! The Holy Spirit has become—for me—a vital part of the whole Christian experience. It is not itself the whole. It is not the totality of the Christian faith. But it is a vital piece of the whole.

The Holy Spirit has moved from being relatively absent to being creatively present in the life of faith. Even in this somewhat enlightened awareness, however, we are sometimes ill at ease with the subject. Many of us are rather wary of persons who are "Spirit filled" or who claim this to be the only authentic posture in life. We balk when someone asks the question, "Is your church a Spirit-filled church?" We are not sure of the language and are suspicious of the questioner's motives. We feel as if we are being judged.

Is this subject another flash in the pan of Christian history? Is it a fad? Is it the beginning of a splinter group in the church? Will it split the church?

United Methodists may occasionally lead the pack in such careful skepticism. The late Halford Luccock used to compare the way in which roof lines are decorated in various denominational traditions. He said that Roman Catholic and Episcopal churches have crosses on their steeples, to remind them of the sacrifice of Christ. Congregational churches have weather vanes on their churches, as a reminder of our democratic heritage. But United Methodist Churches have lightning rods. They were struck by lightning and fire once before, and they want to protect themselves lest it happen again!

We are a bit uneasy.

We know intellectually that the Holy Spirit is integral to our faith, and here biblical scholarship has been helpful. Luke, for example, tells of the Spirit at work throughout his gospel narrative—in the announcement of the birth of John, in the baptism and ministry of Jesus, and, of course, on the day of Pentecost. The Gospel of John refers to the promises regarding the Holy Spirit as "wisdom," as "comforter," as "counselor." And Paul makes many references to the Spirit in his letters to young churches.

Nevertheless, we are not sure how to connect with the spiritual power and presence of the Holy Spirit, or even if we want to.

At this point, we turn our attention to the text for this chapter. In these splendid words we find yet another gracious imperative for the discipleship journey. "If we live by the Spirit, let us also be guided by the Spirit." Let us *live* in the Spirit and let us *walk* by the Spirit.

Open Yourself to the Spirit

First, open up to the Spirit. Open up your life to this reality. Become more receptive. Learn to receive the Spirit into your life.

Many years ago, a very thoughtful lay member of my student pastorate helped me see this clearly. In an adult Sunday school class he taught, he suggested that the Holy Spirit is "the present tense of God." We know God the Creator of the universe. We know Jesus of Nazareth, the One by whom we see and understand the nature and character of God. But the Holy Spirit is God in the present tense. The Spirit is God "now" in my life. In the legacy of this insightful friend, I now know that we need to be more open to that "presentness."

The outward symbol of the Holy Spirit in the liturgy of The United Methodist Church is probably Confirmation. As persons are received into membership in the church for the first time, the minister says, "The Lord defend you with his heavenly grace and by his Spirit confirm you in the faith and fellowship of all true disciples of Jesus Christ."[1] The theology of Confirmation is currently under reconsideration in our tradition, but these words are still in place.

For many years, I have preached and taught about the gifts of the Holy Spirit. Each member of the Body of Christ is constantly given gifts and strength for the building up of that Body and for the work of ministry (see Eph. 4:11-12). Our common task is to identify, cultivate, and call forth those spiritual gifts in one another. There are gifts of teaching, administration, music, care and listening, leadership, and many others. My own theology of leadership in the local church is based on this understanding of spiritual gifts.

But we need more. We need to open ourselves to receive more. We need to learn to receive and appropriate the presence of the Holy Spirit in our lives. The ability to cope and thrive in this life depends on such openness.

A man walked into his pastor's office one day. This man was prominent in his community and in his local church. He announced to his pastor that he had just come from the office of his physician, who had told him that he had a virulent strain of cancer. The doctor gave him the prognosis that he might have six to twelve months to live.

"I have no spiritual resources, no strength to face this," he said. "Some people think I am wealthy. By the world's standards, I suppose I am. But I am poor in the things that count the most."

After a brief pause, he said, "The truth is that I am destitute, spiritually destitute."

He thought for a moment more and then said, "Pastor, do you know that I could walk into any bank in this city and borrow any sum of money I wished just on my name alone? I guess there are some things you just can't borrow."

Without some considerable openness to the Holy Spirit, we are more and more spiritually destitute.

Without that openness, we have no idea how to cope with many of the issues that face us today. The Bible is a marvelous, sacred book. But the Bible does not speak of many of today's concerns. Where in the Bible can you find advice and counsel on abortion or on apartheid? Where does the Bible speak clearly to issues of euthanasia or environmental pollution? Where does the Scripture speak to the issues of surrogate parenthood or teenage suicide? There is very little mention in the Bible of suicide, and it is certainly never specifically condemned.

Only when we are open to the Spirit of God, the "presentness" of God in the world, can we begin to find guidance and direction on these and other matters we face.

Someone has said that we need to have the mind of Christ in the bonds of the Spirit. That's a heavy phrase, but a profound one as well. Only when we have that mind can we begin to fashion a substantive faith by which to live.

Then Walk by the Spirit

We must also be guided to "walk" by the Spirit. "If we live by the Spirit, let us also [walk] by the Spirit."

This is not necessarily some pious stance or super-religious ideal. It is a way of daily living.

My covenant group placed a statement in our covenant that

105

causes most of us to pause and reflect regularly. We covenant that we will yield to the initiatives of the Holy Spirit on a daily basis. Each of us in the group freely admits that he or she is a long way from perfecting this discipline. But we know that God's gracious imperative is to yield to the initiatives of the Holy Spirit in our daily walk.

In the beautiful Pocono mountains of eastern Pennsylvania there is a retreat center called Kirkridge. A number of walking trails abound on the acreage of that center. One of the trails has a sign at the beginning that reads simply, "The Great Walk."

This is the nature of the Christian life journey as well. We are to take the "great walk" of the Spirit daily—for refreshment, for inspiration, for guidance, and for holistic living. We are to take the theology, the connection, and the experience of the Holy Spirit into the world of our daily lives.

Ernest Campbell tells of the day he was in the Metrodome stadium in Minneapolis for a baseball game. He did not enjoy the crowded seats or the blaring speaker system, but he did find a special meaning in the process of exiting the stadium that day:

> When one leaves the Metrodome, there is a mighty push of wind that propels one to the outside world in a hurry. A physicist would be needed to explain this phenomenon. Something about the controlled pressure of the dome clashing with the prevailing pressure outside. But the outrush is strong and unmistakable. It has thrust. It propels. Exiting this sports arena is an event in itself.
>
> What if the Holy Spirit were to thrust us out into the world with a similar force after our "in house worship"? Perhaps we'd be more excited, more animated about the Kingdom.[2]

Is this not what Paul is saying in Galatians 5:25? If we live by the Spirit, let us walk—be guided—by the Spirit.

The imperative, then, is to live as closely to the Spirit as is humanly possible. We assume a posture of disciplined living in dialogue with the Spirit of God. We live closely in order to stay current and to stay on track with our lives.

An Anglican bishop was asked to speak at a Christian conference somewhere in England. For many weeks, he did not respond to the written invitation. Finally, the corresponding secretary for the conference wrote the bishop an insistent note. "We must know," he said, "if you are coming. We need to make our plans."

The bishop wrote back that he was waiting for the guidance of the Holy Spirit on the matter. He would let them know in about four weeks.

The exasperated secretary fired back this letter: "Bishop, please don't bother. Cancel the invitation. We are not interested in having anyone speak at our Conference who lives four weeks away from the Holy Spirit!"[3]

If we *live* by the Spirit, let us *walk* by the Spirit. Let us have the mind of Christ in the bonds of the Spirit.

Notes

---

3. Journey Gently!

1. Sally Graham Ernst, "What Do Children Need for Christmas?" *Response,* November 1989, p. 5.
2. From a leaflet published by the Board of Pensions of The United Methodist Church, fall 1990.

4. Bring Light!

1. "A Time to Seek," *Newsweek,* December 17, 1990, pp. 50-56.

5. Grasp Hope!

1. From a newsletter's pastor's column by the Rev. Don Underwood, Christ United Methodist Church, Plano, Texas, December 7, 1990.
2. Bernie S. Seigel, "How to Heal Yourself," an interview by Mitchell Lodge, *Ladies Home Journal,* June 1989, p. 108.

7. Maintain Vision!

1. From a lecture by David Lowes Watson on January 5, 1991. David Watson is the head of the section on Covenant Discipleship for The United Methodist Church in Nashville, Tennessee.
2. Herb Miller, *The Vital Congregation* (Nashville: Abingdon Press, 1990), pp. 19-20.
3. *Vital Congregations/Faithful Disciples: A Vision for the Church,* The United Methodist Council of Bishops (Nashville: Graded Press, 1990), p. 68.

NOTES

4. Tony Campolo, *The Kingdom of God Is a Party* (Dallas: Word, 1990), pp. 1-9.

8. Cultivate Compassion!

1. Michael J. Christensen, "Our Ministry to Persons with AIDS," *International Christian Digest,* November 1988, p. 16.
2. John Drescher, "Homiletic Miscellany," *Pulpit Digest,* March/April 1988, p. 70.
3. Clyde Chesnutt, "Windows on Preaching," *Circuit Rider,* July/August 1990, p. 19.
4. James Wall, *The Christian Century,* May 30–June 6, 1990, p. 556.

9. Focus Inward!

1. Loraine Hansberry, *A Raisin in the Sun* (New York: Penguin Books, 1988), p. 51.
2. For more information on this special opportunity for Christian discipline, see David Lowes Watson, *Accountable Discipleship,* rev. ed. (Nashville: Discipleship Resources, 1986).

10. Worship Faithfully!

1. Miller, *The Vital Congregation,* p. 28.
2. William Willimon, "Consuming Fire," *Preaching* (September-October 1990): 27.
3. Dietrich Bonhoeffer, *Life Together* (New York: Harper and Bros., 1954), p. 19.
4. William Quick, *Signs of Our Times* (Nashville: Abingdon Press, 1989), pp. 116-17.
5. Miller, *The Vital Congregation,* p. 28.

11. Pursue Perfection!

1. *The Book of Discipline* (Nashville: The United Methodist Publishing House, 1988), p. 232.
2. Joe Paterno with Bernard Asbell, *Paterno by the Book* (New York: Random House, 1989), pp. 14, 17-18.
3. Helmut Thielicke, *I Believe: The Christian's Creed* (Philadelphia: Fortress Press, 1968), p. 7.

4. Dave Dravecky with Tim Stafford, *Comeback* (Grand Rapids: Zondervan, 1990), pp. 217-18.

5. "Record Number of Persons Committed to Christ," *Emerging Trends,* Princeton Research Center, 12, 6, June 1990.

6. The study is reported in *The Christian Century,* May 9, 1990, pp. 496-99.

7. Ibid., p. 496.

8. "Pluralism Is Not a Four-Letter Word," *Circuit Rider,* April 1990, p. 10.

12. Spread Encouragement!

1. From a sermon by Dr. Rodney Wilmoth, St. Paul's United Methodist Church, Omaha, Nebraska.

2. From *In the Christian Spirit* (New York: Herder & Herder, 1969), pp. 95-96.

3. *Vital Congregations/Faithful Disciples: Vision for the Church,* by the United Methodist Council of Bishops (Nashville: Graded Press, 1990), pp. 158-59.

13. Sustain Spirituality!

1. *The Book of Worship for Church and Home* (Nashville: The Methodist Publishing House, 1965), p. 13.

2. Ernest T. Campbell, *Campbell's Notebook,* vol. 10, no. 4, October 1990.

3. Ernest T. Campbell, *Campbell's Notebook,* vol. 10, no. 1, January 1990.